The Day I SAY YES!

Order My Steps Dear God

Elder Jacqueline Coates

Copyright © 2024, Elder Jacqueline Coates All rights reserved.

Contents

INTRODUCTION	8
CHAPTER	15
WHY SHOULD GOD CHOSE ME?	15
CHAPTER 2	23
LET GO AND LET GOD DO IT!	23
CHAPTER 3	32
I AGREED TO SAY "YES"	32
CHAPTER 4	38
REORDER	38
CHAPTER 5	49
DISORDER	49
CHAPTER 6	60
GOD'S PURPOSE	60
CHAPTER 7	69
GOD'S GLORY	69
CHAPTER 8	74
NOAH- GOD'S ENGINEER	74
CHAPTER 9	77
MAN OF FAITH ABRAHAM (ABRAM)	77
CHAPTER 10	83
PAUL GOD'S SPOKESMAN	83
CHAPTER 11	93
ORDER IN PENTECOST	93
CHAPTER 12	103

ORDER YOUR MIND	103
CHAPTER 13	108
ORDER IN OUR HEART	108
CHAPTER 14	113
REJOICE AND CELEBRATE THE NEW YOU	113
CHAPTER 15	119
FINALITY OF GOD'S ORDER REVELATION	119
RESOURCES	124
OTHER BOOKS	125

Foreword

ORDER a small five letter word with huge ramifications and multi-dimensional precision with perspective. In our walk with God and facing life challenges, you will find life's walk and challenges will be less challenging. When operating in order, God in his divine wisdom does everything in order. He operates in order. Seeing that we are created in his image and likeness. Also, given his attributes we must operate to maximize our purpose in the life given to us.

The author of this book like me, we are under the leadership of Bishop Jonathan Wallace Sr. Every year he gives the congregation a specific focus to study and understand the purpose of God for us in this season. This year's focus is "Order My Steps: The Return to Divine Order." My sister in Christ who had authored 6 other books, was inspired to write this book. In reading this book, I find it simplistic yet carries impactful information. Our lives can spiral out of control quickly. The hymnologist says, "Life is full of swift transition." In other words, sometimes life puts us out of order signs. Just as using the GPS and still making a wrong turn. The system will do what is called reentering to make us whole again.

One of my favorite chapters is "Reorder." It is just putting us back in back in order. The book has a wealth of information regarding order, good reading, and sound theological perspective.

It gives you perfect understanding that we serve a God of Order! 1 Corinthians 14:33 says, "For God is not a God of disorder but of Peace as in all meeting of God's Holy people.

This book is so for this time. We are living in a time and life situations that we have never experienced before. I call it Uncharted territory. It can be used as a Biblical compass to navigate your way through life in order and not disorder. ORDERED STEPS!!!

Bishop Dennis Wayne Jefferson

INTRODUCTION

It is my spiritual intention to share with you my new believers, seasoned believers the necessary of allowing and permitting God to daily transform and order your spiritual life. Let us define the word "Order" it means to make firm, establish, to permit, allow. Overall, the Bible portrays God's order as a foundational principle that guides human existence, emphasizing the importance of aligning one's life with God's purposes and designs for the kingdom. These principles and commands are outlined throughout the 66 books of the Holy Bible. God wants an army of believers authorized with his power and filled with his Holy Spirit. So that this fallen evil world can visualize the glorious gospel emanating in their spiritual life. We here at Manna Nation Ministries are given the yearly theme, which is "Order my Steps" The Return to Divine Order by our leader and covering- Dr. Jonathan Wallace Sr., Founder and Senior Pastor.

It is with my sincere desire that as I share the Holy Spirit's revelation and guidance of this theme and book title to aspire and to propel you to seek first to allow God to direct your steps toward the spiritual goal of being righteous. Our theme scripture found in Psalm 37:23 "The steps of a good man are ordered by the Lord, and he delights in his way" A perfect match with the theme we have been given.

Our 1st chapter begins with a thoughtful consideration and your contemplation of "Why Should God Chose Me? I will give you the answers to your query. By using scriptures and spiritual analogies of thought to help you understand the benefits, blessings of being invited to order your lifestyle. Showing you the rewards of an orderly mindset and pure heart. You have potential. You have spiritual stamina. God sees beyond what you see within yourself. God see's your worth, your family or friends may feel indifferent but remember you are accepted by the beloved. How do we know this because in his word, Matthew 3:17 God called his precious, dear Son Jesus, his "beloved.".

I work out in the gym, and I walk a lot, my Fit bit watch tracks my steps every day, one day I completed 7,000 steps. Oh! Yes, this is good for the physical body, but "What are we doing for the inner man? How are we addressing those spiritual deficiencies in our lives? that need to be corrected.

Yes! God wants you to be willing to come to him in this critical hour of change. Yes! when you get your life in order you want to share this awesome change in your life with others. When you hear that quiet voice of God speaking to you and telling you to come follow me, my sister, and my brother, He has spiritual blessings beyond your imagination. This is the time to heed the call and choose to get your spiritual house in order. In Chapter 2 "Let Go! and Let God do it! I show you the importance of letting go of your precious "Self" and permit God to change you and realizing that walking in the flesh is not profitable for your spiritual growth. Giving you questions to consider as you ponder the reality of Letting God have all of "You"

Are you simply ignoring your spiritual imperfections or thinking they will go away? Or are you seeking God and asking him to align your mindset and heart with the principles of the living word of God.

Chapter 3 "I Agree to Say "Yes". The Affirmation that closes the "No" in your flesh, so that the "Yes" in your spirit can be obedient to the voice of God. I share with you my wonderful "Yes" testimony of obedience. I discuss how you can understand his will and divine reasoning in your spiritual life. The importance of you agreeing with his will for your life and how your "Yes" is working for your good. Chapter 4 "Reorder" Brings us to an imperative topic that is "Reorder", where we elaborate on the beginning of creation and the darkness in the earth, which needed God's order. We discuss the fall of Adam and the sin factor how it affected generations of humanity and the remedy for sending His Son Jesus, the Messiah. We discuss the influence of a thinker Rohr, his comments on "Reorder" and how humanity should not just accept faults and imperfections but look to God as their source of healing and restoration. You do not have to stay in the mindset of sinful carnality. God has in his good pleasure a Divine Reorder he wants to create in you that is "A New You" beyond your spiritual imagination. Finally, we introduce you to why you need "Reorder" in your life, it is rewards and benefits of putting on godly virtues as opposed to just settling for what the enemy has to offer you which is eternal separation from God. Chapter 5 "Disorder" Where we describe the world in the past, as it once was a place of justice, equality, and civil order. Giving you definite scriptures proving how the world has backslidden (turned away) from morals and truth. Pinpointing "Disorder" as a depose of holy orders. We truthfully explain that humanity has turned from biblical truths to ungodliness, producing heinous effects in our society. Drawing a Model of God's Order taken from the scriptures for believers to follow. Chapter 6 "God's Purpose" God's purpose for humanity was initiated because he loved humankind and designed a remedy for his salvation. As outlined in his 66 books written by holy men of God inspired by the Holy Spirit.

Chapter 7 "God's Glory" The constancy of Jesus Christ reflects God's unchanging order. This glory involves us taking time to spend time in his presence, or when we study his word and abide in his word, we learn about the truth of his glory. The more we take time to meditate and study his word we allow order in our life; the holy word begins to transform us working through the power of the Holy Spirit. When God sees an ordered and unified body of believers offering up praises and worship to him, he is being glorified. Hallelujah

Chapter 8 "Noah-God's Engineer" God ordered Noah's steps, he gave him the blueprint for the massive building of the ark and the finality of his ordered task was secured with the Noahic Covenant. In Genesis 6:18 "But with thee will I establish my covenant; and thou shalt come into the ark, thou, and thy sons, and thy wife, and thy sons' wives with thee." Chapter 9 "Man of Faith-Abraham" This was Abraham's true test of faith in the God that he walked with. God responded Genesis 18:14 "Is anything too hard for the Lord? At the time appointed I will return unto thee, according to the time of life, and Sarah shall have a son." Abraham was taught great patience, he desired to have a son, so that all he possessed would be inherited by him. God established the Abrahamic Covenant with him that was a sign and a token of being everlasting. Chapter 10 "Paul-God's Spokesman" We have been sharing with you our readers and believers the importance of ordering your steps with our heavenly Father God. At times we may choose a path decided on by our own intellect assuming that this way is right. However, there was one man Saul, of Tarsus, (Paul) who was a highly educated man, who was aggressively ordered to change for God's chosen assignment. Chapter 11 "Order in Pentecost" In the book of Acts it declares the historical beginnings of the early church on the day of Pentecost. Chapter 12 "Order in your Mind" Just because you are comfortable with your lifestyle, it does not make it ok. The things that you may be following or participating in may not be giving God glory, only giving you temporary pleasure. Chapter 13 "Order in your Heart" When our spiritual heart is filled with all kinds of wickedness and sinfulness it produces hardness to hearing the voice of the living God. We are to concentrate on being sensitive to the voice of God. Chapter 14 "Rejoice and Celebrate the new You" You have a new sense of happiness, you can now rejoice, the spirit of joy is resting on you, because you have chosen to allow God's hand to touch you. You have taken all of your past and laid it aside, all your sins are forgiven, the weight and burden are no more upon your heart. Your mind is renewed, your heart is changed, and you are walking in the will of God. Chapter 15 "Finality of God's Order Revelation" "The Day I say "Yes" Order my Steps Dear God. It has been a wonderful literary journey that has opened our theme from Manna Nation Ministries for the new year of 2024, Order my Steps-

A Return to Divine Order. We have traveled the path of Order and discussed the many foundations of how God can miraculously rearrange and change individuals for his divine will and purpose. Humanity's destination has a beginning and an ending, which we have discussed in our chapters, and why order is necessary in one's spiritual life. Follow God's steps, stay in the correct path, obedience is the reward of final and awesome blessing, which is fulfilling our ultimate desire to spend eternity with our Lord.

CHAPTER 1

WHY SHOULD GOD CHOSE ME?

Why should God choose me? You have potential. You have spiritual stamina. God sees beyond what you see within yourself. God see's your worth, your family or friends may feel indifferent but remember you are accepted by the beloved. How do we know this because in his word, Ephesians 1:6 'To the praise of the glory of his grace, wherein he hath made us accepted in the beloved." And also in Matthew 3:17 God called his precious, dear Son Jesus, his "beloved".

God sent his precious Son, Jesus to redeem you and show you all his promises that are written in the Bible. Yes! you are the one that God wants to change and order your life.

Jesus during his public ministry in biblical times of the New Testament used his eleven disciples to further this great act of evangelism in the earth. According to the great commission of Jesus, (Matthew 28:19) he summoned and commanded his eleven disciples to teach all nations the wonderful gospel and observe its commandments. From these nations were to come new believers who would be his leaders, missionaries, evangelists, teachers to carry and further the good news of Jesus the "gospel."

God so desires orderly and anointed people like you to do his will. Yes! God wants you to be willing to come to him in this critical hour of change. God wants you first to be filled with his Holy Spirit, filled with his" (in Greek "dunamis) meaning power in action. Yes! in Acts 1:8 "But ye shall receive power after the Holy Ghost is come upon you: and ye shall be witnesses unto me both in Jerusalem, and in all Judea, and in Samaria, and unto the uttermost part of the earth".

As you grow in faith and grow in his word, your light in you will get brighter and brighter. That is, letting his light. shine through you to be that spiritual magnet to draw souls. to the kingdom. Yes! when you get your life in order, you. will be excited to share this formidable change in your life with others.

God will start and continue an excellent work in you. I love this verse of scripture in Philippians 1:6 "Being confident of this very thing, that he which hath begun a good work in you will perform it until the day of Jesus Christ".

When you hear that quiet voice of God speaking to you and telling you to come follow him, my sister, and my brother, know that I have spiritual blessings beyond your imagination. This is the time to heed the call and choose to get your spiritual house in order.

Things may not be the way you want them, family relationships are upset, you have financial problems, your children are not being obedient but listen this is the time to accept God's invitation to put things in spiritual order. No other means will do it, because when God does the work in your life, you are new in him. It says so in II Corinthians 5:17 "Therefore if any man be in Christ, he is a new creature: old things are passed away: behold all things are become new". Why would you not want the abundant life God has for you. My mother had a saying "don't sell yourself short." She was telling me put some value on your life, be confident about who you can be in God. God see's your value, he knows what you can do as long as you walk by faith in him. It may take time, it may take a moment, but realize as time progresses, you will notice the chaos will turn into peace, the confusion will be gone.

You have chosen now to be led by his Holy Spirit. Yes! the Holy Spirit is for you, it's for your salvation, healing and deliverance. Yes!s Be willing to surrender and let the hand of God lead you toward the destiny he has for you. Do not be afraid. In Romans 8:28 (paraphrase) God is doing his work in your life for your spiritual good and his purpose. When your life is in order it is not hard to surrender, because now you are walking in spiritual freedom. You are no longer under bondage to the rudiments and cares of the world.

Colossians 2:8 "Beware lest any man spoil you through philosophy and vain deceit, after the tradition of men, after the rudiments of the world, and not after Christ." The world's philosophy contaminates your mindset to believe that these customs and societal norms are ok or acceptable. But if these things oppose the word of God, they are only leading one's life astray. If we want to continue to have an ordered life, you must guard the portals of our soul, our spirit and our mind. Keeping his pure word as treasures in our heart.

The Psalmist was right by professing Psalm 119:105 "Thy word is a lamp unto my feet, and a light unto my path." Persist and Pursue to keep your mindset to clearly hear his voice to do his will. Yes! you have the spiritual capabilities to succeed in your spiritual journey. Do not believe the lies of the enemy, Satan. He wants to deter you from progressing in holiness. Don't let his voice whisper phony truths of his promises in your ear. Stop entertaining his false lies. All he wants is to rob your soul. Satan does not mean you good, because wickedness and evil works of darkness are the fruit of his deceitfulness.

In John 10:10 it clearly states, "The thief (Satan) cometh not, but for to steal and to kill, and to destroy: I am come that they might have life, and that they might have it more abundantly."

Satan's plans and purpose Is to Seek you to:

- Steal

- Kill

- Destroy

God has a plan and a purpose for you. In Jeremiah 29:11 he declares "For I know the thoughts that I think toward you, saith the LORD, thoughts of peace, and not of evil, to give you an expected end." Do you not realize that God already predestined you for this major order of life changing virtues. God has crafted a spiritual design for each of his individuals who chose to allow his hand to order their steps. Do you not know you are predestined for his will? The word "predestined" means "election of all who are saved." When you align your will with his will you bring in His divine order. You know what happens, expect all kinds of blessings to begin to pour into your life. The world has many elections and people must choose ballots of their choice, the outcome has to be tallied and the winner with the most votes win. These folk think they have resumes to prove that they are qualified. But God's spiritual pedigree is quite different.

Romans 8:30-31 it states, "Moreover whom he did predestinate, them he also called: and whom he called, them he also justified: and whom he justified, them he also glorified."

What shall we then say to these things? If God be for us, who can be against us?" Who but God can do a spiritual makeover in your life and giving you abundant life in Christ.

God's FREE GIFTS TO YOU!

·   You are Predestined — elected.

·   You are Called — pleasurable invitation.

·   You are Justified — He moved you from injustice to a state of grace and righteousness.

·   You are Glorified — ultimate step of redemption.

·   God's — Good pleasure

God already knows beforehand who he wanted. God's spiritual requirements of order have eternal rewards. God had you in his mind, to choose you, to call you, he was praying for you to answer his voice with a "Yes."

God has a better way, a glorious way and a peaceful way ending in an orderly way. The world cannot guarantee this, oh no they can't say this choice that you made is one that results in good. The world is governed by the course of evil and false truths. When you choose to allow your heart to be filled with dreadful things, the fruit of this is evil works.

Look at what God wants to give you in Luke 12:32 "Fear not, little flock; for it is your Father's good pleasure to give you the kingdom." It is God's good pleasure to give you the kingdom. God's wants to work in you a course of his divine order. Philippians 2:13 "For it is God which worketh in you both to will and do of his good pleasure." Another act of God's divine calling on your life. In II Thessalonians 1:11 "Wherefore also we pray always for you, that our God would count you worthy of this calling, and fulfill all the good pleasure of his goodness, and the work of faith with power."

God's expectation of you is worth and value you are special in his eyes, as Pastor Meyers in my church declares to us. When you chose to accept God's way of order, you are denying that you will not allow chaotic people, situations, or lifestyles govern your spiritual life. When you humbly submit to Jesus Christ, you will experience peace that passes all understanding, because now you are living by his Word and allowing the Holy Spirit to teach you and to guide you into an ordered life of truth and righteousness.

Instead of saying "Why" say "Lord help me to stay in obedience and be still, trusting in you every day for my new ordered life.

CHAPTER 2

LET GO AND LET GOD DO IT!

This word "Let" is a powerful action verb. It means to not prevent, or forbid, but to allow. Sometimes the things that we deem precious to us may bring temporary gratification, and yet cause a series of discontent or grief. At times, we are in between a decision to let go of our problems and difficulties. To not be the one to fix them, but surrendering to the will of God, Let him do it.

When Jesus was walking along the sea of Galilee, he saw Simon and Andrew his brother casting a net into the sea. Both men had an occupation of being fishers. Jesus next action was calling them to put aside your nets and Follow me, and I will make you fishers of men. They immediately left their nets and followed Jesus. (Matthew 4:17-20). Now let us surmise this situation. Did these two men have a lucrative business catching fish? I really don't believe they did, because had it been the case they would have questioned who he was and then stated why we should leave what we have. But, later in (Mark 10:23-31) Peter confessed we have left all. It is possible from the confession of Peter they may have been slightly rich. When Jesus choose and called his disciples, they had occupations and had reputations in their communities.

Yet, when Jesus started his public ministry, he needed people who would be committed and dedicated for the work of his ministry. Jesus knew each one of them, good points, and their bad dispositions. Yes! he knew even that one of them would betray him, yet he was included in his inner circle. The twelve disciples were inquisitive about Jesus and his ministry. They wanted more than what they had in the past and ran to be with him. They were willing to let go of all they held dear to themselves and follow Jesus.

God wants to give you an opportunity to welcome change, he wants you to experience the orderly transformation in your spiritual life to bring order. But you must partner with him to orchestrate spiritual change. Do it like this verse commands. Romans 12:1 "I beseech you brethren by the mercies of God that you present your bodies a living sacrifice, holy, acceptable unto God, which is your reasonable service."

It will take total surrender, denial of cries of your flesh, while crucifying those unholy desires and committing to your eternal "Yes." Leaving behind your carnal desires, your fleshly ways, doubts, worries, and fears. Confessing that Jesus is Lord and Master of your life and acknowledging God's "omniscience," his all possessing knowledge. If your natural life is full of chaos, disorder, mayhem, it's time for a change. The cycle needs to be broken, the chains need to be loosed and your heart needs to be lifted from the heavy burdens.

When you laid yourself on the altar, you are letting God put his majestic hands on you to produce a glorious masterpiece. This masterpiece is you being changed and ordered. You can be his handiwork of outstanding artistry and workmanship. If the God of our universe could create such explicit creations for the world to adore, why not allow his handiwork to prevail in your spiritual life. God wants to take the bad, the ugly, broken parts of you and change you. II Corinthians 5:17 "Therefore if any man be in Christ, he is a new creature: old things are passed away; behold, all things are become new." When you are a new person in Christ, we become his and we strive to not yield to serve the enemy nor practice sin. We are Christ's beholding workmanship Ephesians 2:10 "For we are his workmanship, created in Christ Jesus unto good works, which God hath before ordained that we should walk in them" How do you walk in his works? God helps us by his genuine grace for salvation. God wants us to be filled with fruits of righteousness. Do you not know that when you are filled with something, there is no room for anything else to be put in it. According to Philippians 1:11 "Being filled with the fruits of righteousness, which are by Jesus Christ, unto the glory and praise of God." You are becoming a masterpiece reflecting his image of righteousness, which in turn helps you to live a holy life. That consecrated, dedicated holy life authorizes you to defeat works of darkness and bind and lose evil attacks. You become a warrior to fight this good fight of faith.

I Timothy 6:12 "Fight the good fight of faith, lay hold on eternal life. whereunto thou art also called, and hast professed a good profession before many witnesses." Your family is watching, your friends are expecting you to win this battle. This orderly life is an eternal profession rewarding the believer with many spiritual blessings.

Be more determined to walk by faith and not by sight. God wants you to decree and declare all the promise of the New Covenant in the New Testament books of the Bible.

As you follow Christ in your ordered life, read in your Bible over 7,000 promises of good things that God wants to fulfill in you. God wants you to trust him, God wants you to have good health, God wants your family saved. God wants you free, and to not be oppressed or depressed or living in anxiety.

God designed so many promises for us, they are ours, if we believe it. God recorded them and established them as his divine agreement. God wants his believers to enjoy the fruitful benefits of them. Knowing this great revelation, it persuades one to love this God of order, provoking us to live an orderly life. Loving God with all our being as declared in Matthew 22:37 "Jesus said unto him, Thou shalt love the Lord thy God with all thy heart, and with all thy soul, and with all thy mind."

When Jesus was walking through the land of Jericho, there was a man named Zachaeus, this man was an important official a "chief" of the publicans, a rich man. This man was a tax collector, a very despicable occupation, yet he was seeking to find something or someone who could deliver him. He had no friends, he was a liar, a false accuser, taking more than he deserved. The Jews hated him because he worked for Rome. Zachaeus had a condemning conscience, ridden with guilt. Yet, Jesus gave him a humble invitation to "Come." In Luke 19:1-10 (verse 5) "And when Jesus came to the place, he looked up, and saw him, and said unto him, "Zachaeus, make haste, and come down for today I must abide at thy house". Jesus was a soul seeker, Jesus was a healer, appearances did not matter, the soul mattered. Jesus was there to show this sinner, a new and living way, a fresh new path to follow. In Luke 19:9-10 "And Jesus said unto him, This day is salvation come to this house, for so much as he also is a son of Abraham. For the Son of man is come to seek and to save that which was lost." A lost soul that was given an order of salvation for him and those of his household. Zachaeus had come to a sincere decision to turn from his evil ways. He was willing to Let go! and Let God. He was willing to let go of his greed for money and accept salvation to change his heart and his ways. When we chose to forgive ourselves for the terrible mistakes we have made, it is then that we can experience God's mercy and grace.

Yes, we messed up big time, but we serve a forgiving God, who does not sit somewhere counting our wrongdoings. When we humbly admit and confess our sins, he is faithful and just to forgive us. I John 1:9 If we confess our sins, he is faithful and just to forgive us our sins, and to cleanse us from all unrighteousness." The word "If" is a conditional clause relating to a situation or a condition, it's based on your decision to do it or not.

When you chose to do something the right way, you will be rewarded. The forgiveness that Jesus renders brings peace and joy to our souls. Yes! We have to let go of that brick of pride, which keeps us in bondage, which refuses to humble our "self.' When we refuse to take advantage of spiritual opportunities to change and say I do not trust this, I'm not going to take this chance, and you repeat in your mind, it's not going to work for my good. You are not taking advantage of God's grace. What you are saying is not worth my time and my effort. The problem is you are emotionally damaged goods, and this is the season for you to order your steps. God can heal you mentally and emotionally. God is willing to heal you. Psalm 147:3 "He health the broken in heart, and bindeth up their wounds." You are crying, spiritually bleeding, let the God of compassion, the God of love, Jehovah-Rope Heal you and make you whole. Jeremiah 33:6 "Behold, I will bring it health and cure, and I will cure them and will reveal unto them abundance of peace and truth."

God wants to give you hope that true peace, God wants to order a miracle for you. When you say "Yes" are you willing to "Let Go" and Let God, are you confessing your faith in God and not struggling in your own power. Some things you have no control over, those things turn them over to God. In I Peter 5:6-7 "Humble yourselves therefore under the mighty hand of God, that he may exalt you in due: Casting all your care upon him; for he careth for you." Pray and ask God not to let your pride get in the way of your spiritual progress. You can choose scriptures to meditate on to keep your mind on Christ. One thing do not let the spirit of fear dominate your emotions. If you hear unwelcome news, don't say "Oh, I'm next" change you thinking to something joyful.

In II Timothy 1:7 "For God hath not given us the spirit of fear; but of power, and of love and of a sound mind." Do not let your mind be confused with all the negativity and bad news, that troubles you and prevents from focusing on God's will for you. God is creating the new you, each day you are moving in new levels of grace, new spiritual maturity and acquiring new wisdom and knowledge.

Giver of the riches of His Glory

- He is your Father of Glory

- Spirit of Wisdom

- Revelation in the knowledge in Him

- Understanding being enlightened.

- Hope of His calling

- Riches of His Glory of His Inheritance

- Greatness of His Power

- Working of his mighty Power

My treasure chest verse In Ephesians 1:17-19 "That the God of our Lord Jesus Christ, the Father of glory, may give unto you the spirit of wisdom and revelation in the knowledge of him: The eyes of your understanding being enlightened; that ye may know what is the hope of his calling, and what the riches of the glory of his inheritance in the saints, And what is the exceeding greatness of his power to us-ward who believe, according to the working of his mighty power."

Celebrate the majesty of our God and the spiritual deposits that he will give you when you totally and freely Let Go and Let God do it." God wants you to believe that he can, and he will prepare you for that new orderly life in Him.

CHAPTER 3

I Agreed to Say "Yes"

In our lives sometimes, things do not go the way we anticipate or planned. We tend to lean on our own intellect to make decisions, but the truth be told God in his majesty and His wonderful insight has something far better for us. I remember when I was minding my own business and God came along and told me to complete a spiritual assignment. I say, "Who Me," and he say yes "You." Well! He instructed me as to what to do and what to say. The problem was I had already said "No." God distinctly gave me a vision of an event and he showed me the person in the vision. Well! One Sunday morning the service was really in that Manna Nation worship mode; God spoke to me and said, "Go Now" and I was silent. God told me two more times and said he would chasten me if I was disobedient. Oh No! I did not want that, not from our God.

I agreed to Say "Yes." Oh yes, I was trembling in my shoes, but I did what God commanded. That incident with God taught me a lesson, not to be disobedient.

Since then, I have humbly submitted to do all he commands me to do. I give you, my readers, my personal testimony to encourage you not to miss your spiritual opportunity. God called me and chose me for his glory. To be his Prophet for the work of the ministry.

I can gladly report that since that inception many have been blessed. I want you the believers of the living God to know that nothing is impossible for you when God is with you. God will take you through open doors when you say "Yes." Your willingness to agree with the plans of God are not only for you individually, but yielding brings blessing for your entire household. When you totally commit to God in your spiritual relationship, you will experience the victory over all the power of the enemy Satan. You have been given authority, Matthew 18:18 "Verily I say unto you, Whatsoever ye shall bind on earth shall be bound in heaven: and whatsoever ye shall loose on earth shall be loosed in heaven." When you find yourself threatened or under attack by the enemy, Satan, you have the necessary tools to defeat the enemy. God is ordering your steps for his glory and his good pleasure.

The word "authority" is the power or right to give orders, make decisions and enforce obedience. Who do you think you have the power to order? I am glad you asked Satan, his demons, his cohorts, witches, wizards, warlocks and whoever else operates in the kingdom of darkness. Now you have the God given right to order the enemy, Satan to bow down at the name of Jesus. The God given authority to plead the blood against him and send him back to the abyss.

The abyss is the place of demons, a prison, the sheol, the realm of rebellious spirits.

When you live by God's commandments, God's holy scriptures and apply them to your life, the results are powerful against the spiritual world of darkness. When we say "Yes" to God, we no longer allow our will to dominate but we accept His will. We acknowledge Jesus as Lord and Master of our spiritual life. We humbly follow Jesus example as he was a servant and willing to serve with love as outlined in John 13:13-15 and in many other ways during his glorious ministry.

Our "Yes" responds to his grace, it responds to him because we have a heart of gratitude, not a heart full of attitude. We learn each day in our walk with him as he orders our steps to be obedient. We may not understand how or what he is doing in us and through us, but we continue to obey by following his endeavors for our spiritual lives. His Divine Order in your life suggests that you subject your mindset to agree to the terms and conditions of our salvation.

Anytime you sign for a product, for a service or a purchase, the seller asks you to check the box ☑ indicating that you agree with all the terms and conditions. They want to be assured that you understand your decision and your affirmation is willing. God is not pressuring you to serve him or to obey him, he does want you to freely commit to obedience. We are no longer under the dark side of sin; God has translated you into the kingdom of his dear Son.

In Colossians 1:13-14 "Who hath delivered us from the power of darkness, and hath translated us into the kingdom of his dear Son: In whom we have redemption through his blood, even the forgiveness of sins." Praise Jesus and give him the glory. When you chose to be baptized in his name and filled with his precious Holy Spirit speaking in tongues. You are taking the first ordered step.

In Matthew 6:33 "Seek ye first the kingdom of God, and his righteousness, and all these things shall be added to you." We are daily allowing Jesus to change us, Yes, when we were baptized in Jesus name, we were resurrected, meaning we came up from that dead life of sin to a new and living way in Jesus. Our past is left buried, dead, and by faith we live and walk in the newness of this ordered life of salvation. You do not have to figure it out, it's God's transforming work in you for his glory. You now have a testimony of victory, that your belief, your faith has put you in a new status and a new position in his kingdom. You are now a servant of righteousness, yes, take time to read it for yourself its proof of your affirmation. As God arranges and redirects your life, you may find yourself in a struggle between the flesh and the spirit. Know that the key to breaking a particular unholy desire. Is to allow the fruit of the Spirit, which is temperance, or self-control to rule and govern your flesh. You have the faith and power to believe that Christ is in you the hope of glory.

In Romans 8:10 "If Christ be in you, the body is dead because of sin, but the Spirit is life because of righteousness."

I believe this revelation, walk by faith in it every day of your new life in Christ. The worst is behind you, you are no longer a servant of sin, imprisoned to drugs, lust, pride, hatred, habits, and addictions and all kinds of evil works. When you follow the voice of the Holy Spirit and choose to walk in the spirit, there is no room for the above darkness. All you want to do is please Jesus because you cherish your spiritual freedom in Christ. In John 8:36 "If the Son (Jesus) therefore shall make you free, ye shall be free indeed." You have the power through the Holy Spirit to crucify the flesh and live free from a lifestyle of sin.

Now, we could continue about your setbacks, your frustrations, your hurts, but it is our intention to help you to be encouraged and look beyond these situations. We want you to know that you can trust God and cast your cares on him, while he is doing a good work in you. I Peter 5:7 Get your spiritual release "Casting all your care upon him; for he careth for you." Worry is a burden and a spiritual weight on your mind. How can you spiritually progress as God orders your life if your mind is on the problem and not trusting God. As we use our prayer ministry God will render his peace that passeth all understanding. In Philippians 4:7 "And the peace of God, which passeth all understanding, shall keep your hearts and minds through Christ Jesus."

The peace of God will guard your heart so that no worries or anxieties will come into heart. God wants you to have a joyful heart, not a sad heart. So, while God is ordering your steps, "Set" your mind to think on good things, as described in Philippians 4:8 "Finally, brethren, whatsoever things are true, whatsoever things are honest, whatsoever things are just, whatsoever things are pure, whatsoever things are lovely, whatsoever things are of good report; if there be any virtue, and if there be any praise, think on these things." As God directs you into a new spiritual life. You choose thoughts of a high moral standard, as you praise and thanking him for his good grace. As God instructs you in your next step, listen, obey, follow, and watch God do an exceedingly great work in you.

In Ephesians 3:20 "Now unto him that is able to do exceeding abundantly above all that we ask or think, according to the power that worketh in us," You can be that powerful obeying solider in God's army. Your destiny is designed for you. You will understand by and by. God loves you and because you say "Yes" know that his light in you will be a witness for the world, your family and friends will notice the change in your life. Your ordered life is for His Glory so that they can come to know the Christ in you, your hope of glory.

CHAPTER 4

REORDER

God's order is evident in the creation of the planet earth, Yet, God had to reorder the earth, due to imbalance of nature. The word reorder means "rearrange again" or put in order again. Genesis 1:1-2 gives us firsthand knowledge of the existence of planet earth. "In the beginning God created the heaven and the earth. And the earth was without form, and void; and darkness was upon the face of the deep, And the spirit of God moved upon the face of the waters."

Yet. Somewhere between the earth having no form, being void and filled of darkness, God saw a necessary reorder a rearrangement.

God Rearrange the planet earth

- No form

- Void

- Full of Darkness

There and then it was needful for a change amidst the (3) characteristics of the planet earth no form, void and darkness that existed and had to be corrected.

The earth had no significant shape, it was empty, and its appearance was darkness. The darkness has no recognizable objects, and no beauty. Henceforth God begin by speaking the word "Let" (13) times calling forth his divine creation. God brought what did not exist into existence, the elements of nature and animals.

God in all his majesty and infinite wonders created all things in heaven and in earth. God made in his image (2) sin free human beings, Adam from the dust of the earth and Eve from the rib of Adam. (Genesis 1:26-28) (Genesis 2:21-25). In this beautiful oasis, in which there was no sin, suffering, or death, God's human beings were commanded and authorized by God, to rule over His new creation as benevolent stewards. God in loving intention and marvelous design created a utopia that would be befitting for his creation man and woman to live in. I am explaining this in detail so you the reader can understand why Reorder is necessary.

Adam was created in the image of God; they were commanded not to eat of the tree of knowledge of good and evil. (Genesis 2:16-17). But, because, the enemy, serpent, Satan talked to Eve, he persuaded her to doubt God and to think that God was hiding something from them. She in turn took the fruit to Adam and he did eat, and both their eyes were opened. (Genesis 3:7) God was not pleased with what he visualized. Now, since the fall of Adam and Eve, their disobedience warranted God providing a remedy for their sin.

(Romans 5:14) which caused the sin factor to affect generations of humanity. In Genesis 3:15 God revealed His plan to defeat Satan and offer salvation to the world through Jesus. Therefore, we have in Genesis 3:15 our first promise of a Redeemer and a stream of prophecies concerning the coming Messiah. Jesus paid our penalty for sin so that we would have access by faith into this great grace of God. Since the inception of sin, wickedness, evil works and all kinds of false doctrines have filtered societal arenas. This has caused the total disobedience of humanity, turning from the standard of truth and morality. God sent his preachers and prophets to persuade wicked men by sending warnings to judge humanity for their disobedience. Before, Jesus ascended he commanded his disciples to go in all the world and preach. In Matthew 28:19-20 "And Jesus came and spake unto them, saying, All power is given unto me in heaven and in earth. Go ye therefore, and teach all nations, baptizing them in the name of the Father, and of the Son, and of the Holy Ghost. Teaching them to observe all things whatsoever I have commanded you: and, lo, I Am with you always, even unto the end of the world." Peter, the apostle carried the message of repentance as well, in Acts 2:38 "Then Peter said unto them, Repent, and be baptized every one of you in the name of Jesus Christ for the remission of sins, and ye shall receive the gift of the Holy Ghost.

I am laying the foundation so that you my reader can understand the importance of Ordering your steps and having a spiritual relationship of obedience with Jesus Christ. God wants to put his mastery touch on your life so that your entire being is changed, that is your spiritual, mental and emotional life. God is omniscience "all knowing" he knows what is in your heart and how to change your life, he knows your past, present and your future. God can teach you how to live holy.

God's desire is that humanity would accept salvation, healing, and deliverance, so that they too can enjoy the fruits of abundant life. When you affirm your willingness to accept his orders in your life, you are believing and trusting him in his will and actions. Now is the time to ask yourself a serious question, should you, or will you continue in sin? In Romans 6:1 "What shall we say then? Shall we continue in sin, that grace may abound? God is giving you the answer. Romans 6:2 "God forbid. How shall we that are dead to sin, live any longer therein? Humanity needs to ask for a change, a rearrangement in their life, a desire to not walk and live by the sin nature. There are pertinent truths that we must follow as believers so that our spiritual growth will manifest righteous living. It warrants that we do things differently than the world. We must set the bar higher; live a higher standard than the world. The word of God instructs us to put on the new man, why would you want to wear old dirty, ragged clothes that don't benefit your appearance?

The same rule applies when you put on virtues of righteousness, you are now a child of God, representing and what you speak and live. If you are taking the time to hear, your soul shall live. You are yielding so that you can learn the ways of God and the truths you hear, it means you are obeying, Don't be deceived for the word says in James 1:22 "But be ye doers of the word and not hearers only, deceiving your own selves." Why would you waste valuable time and not take God's precious words put them in action, apply them to your spiritual life. When you create something, you must follow the instructions so that you can bring forth a beautiful product. As you do what his word commands you are creating a new person, a renewed person, a transformed person that is acceptable to God. Romans 12:1-2 "I beseech you therefore, brethren, by the mercies of God that ye present your bodies a living sacrifice, holy, acceptable unto God, which is your reasonable service. And be not conformed to this world: but be ye transformed by the renewing of your mind, that ye may prove what is that good and acceptable, and perfect will of God" The word "beseech" (I beg you, you need to do it much) There may come a time when you feel like you have to resist, and you go your own way and make a mess of things. You cannot see the end results now because the way you have chosen is a walk of faith. You must be persuaded in your mind that what you are experiencing is the plan and purpose of God. You can't listen to the many voices that tell you, "Stop" or "Don't go any further"

Listen to the logic, you have to start all over again, you lose time, and you lose spiritual progress. Question your decision, is this for the worse or for the better. Do you believe this to be true of the Lord? or some type of game. Are you willing to receive his divine instructions for life and believe those instructions to be the absolute best for you?

I was researching this title for "Reorder" and came across this infamous teacher of thought, Father Richard Rohr, a Franciscan religious leader, This is his quote and comment "Rohr argues, we must learn to live in appreciation of the shadow lands: that is, to accept our own faults and imperfections as well as those of our institutions and culture. Rohr teaches not to acquiesce but rather to understand their functions and their power in our lives so realistically that we are able to transform ourselves out of their grip. Why would an individual continue to accept living a lifestyle of sin that only brings gloom and spiritual death. The book of Romans gives us an answer, Romans 7:24 "O wretched man that I am! who shall deliver me from the body of this death?" Rohr, didn't know the truth of the scriptures. No one, not even in humanity has the means to redeem themselves, that is why God sent his Son, Jesus who took on the form of a servant to die for all humanity. He was nailed to the cross and shed his blood to pay for our sins, we had no way of doing this. God looked throughout the earth and searched over for someone to save us and redeem us.

There was no one humanly perfect, guiltless, sinless to pay the penalty for our sins. I remember when I was twenty years old, and I had a pack of Newport cigarettes smoking them, I took the cigarette and looked at it, and said to myself "I am tired of living in sin," there is no pleasure in this life, it only lasts a little while. That is when I decided to return back to God. I made my decision to return to God to the spiritual things that brought me lasting joy. How did this happen? I listened to the voice of the devil and followed the wrong path; my steps were in a backslidden state. All I wanted was my way, it was the highway of darkness. I acquiesce meaning "I didn't fight against the temptation" But you know what sin will beat you down, steal your peace and rob you of your joy. I say all this to let you know that I had made up in my mind that this prodigal daughter needed a drastic change in her life. Since, that rude awakening, I made a sincere declaration that I would not, should not, could not leave ever, God again. The Lord has been blessing me so much, that I am profoundly grateful. I am daily learning to crucify my flesh so that I hinder not my spiritual growth and allow new levels that God wants to permit in my life.

I have learned to pray daily, determined to not let certain evil ways be a part of my spirit. I have the keys to the kingdom and those doors are shut and locked in Jesus name.

I use daily Matthew 18:18 "Verily I say unto you, Whatsoever ye shall bind on earth shall be bound in heaven: and whatsoever ye shall loose on earth shall be loosed in heaven." What are you binding and loosing? You are binding these things in Ephesians 6:12 "For we wrestle not against flesh and blood, but against principalities, against powers, against the rulers of the darkness of this world, against spiritual wickedness in high places." There is a lyric in a song that Tasha Cobb sings "use your tool," You have the tool of authority and the power to bind principalities, powers, rulers of darkness and spiritual wickedness. When you have the Holy Ghost on the inside of you, you are already equipped to do spiritual warfare. God wants to help you to reorder your life. It may take you forgiving yourself, yes, you may have messed up, but know that we serve a forgiving and loving God. God wants you to put on new ways, new thinking patterns, and a new heart. God will help you as his elect to this in Jesus name, Colossians 3:12-13 "Put on therefore as the elect of God, holy and beloved, bowels of mercies, kindness, humbleness of mind, meekness, longsuffering: Forbearing one another, and forgiving one another, if any man have a quarrel against any: even as Christ forgave you, so also do ye."

When I studied scriptures regarding the phrase "put on," it implies that one must get rid of old life patterns and put on the new life virtues and applied principles.

It is similar to putting on clothes, if you are going to a nice event, you wouldn't want to go in a dirty dress. So, you take of the dirty dress and put on that fabulous dress, because you want to have a good appearance. Well, my brothers and sisters in Christ: know when God comes for his church the bride, the body of Christ, he will certainly turn his head if he sees a spotted church, a body of believers full of sin and wickedness. Do you think for once you are going to heaven like that? Oh! No! You will need to do some renovating, some remodeling, some changing of spiritual attire.

Order your steps for God's better spiritual rewards. You will receive a crown, your name is written in the Lamb's Book of Life, you have a new home in heaven, the new Jerusalem and so much more. When Christ shall appear, you shall appear with him in glory. Hallelujah! So, it would be to your spiritual advantage to seek those things that are pleasing to your Lord and Savior Jesus Christ. Colossians 3:1-2 "If ye then be risen with Christ, seek those things which are above, where Christ sitteth on the right hand of God. Set your affection on things above, not on things of the earth." The word "Put" in Greek translated "endyo" means "sink into." Paul was emphasizing that when you do this, sinking in, you become rooted in these virtues. Your inner man can change for God's glory resulting in you becoming sanctified.

This word sanctification in Greek "hagiasmos" make holy, to consecrate, to separate from the world, set apart from sin in "Order" that we have close fellowship with God. We want to serve him in Spirit and in truth. When you purchase a car, you must maintain its usage so that you can have it for a long time. It is not an option, it is a mandatory requirement. You get your oil changed, buy new tires after certain miles, get your emission check, so many other things that are necessary. In taking your time to study his word, to pray, you must maintain a lifestyle of holiness. You must choose to get certain things in order when they are out of order.

This calls for you to "work" out" the saving of your soul Philippians 2:12 "Wherefore, my beloved, as ye have always obeyed, not as in my presence only, but now much more in my absence, work out your own salvation with fear and trembling." We are not living right to please our leaders, but to please our Lord. Our leaders don't see us every single day, yet we discipline our flesh to crucify it, walking by faith, and not by sight. Paul admonish us in Colossians 2:5 "For though I be absent in the flesh, yet am I with you in the spirit, joying and beholding your order, and the steadfastness of your faith in Christ."

God wants us to adhere to his godly order. it shows our spiritual maturity and brings joy to your Savior. By doing a spiritual checkup, you are staying ready and prepared to meet God when he calls for his church the "body of believers.

Chose to continue to obey the word of God daily and to be found pleasing in God's eyes. Diligently chose to abstain from things of the world that cause condemnation or guilt. Know that when you chose to separate yourself from ungodliness, you are consciously aligning your will with God's will.

In II Corinthians 6:18 "And will be a Father unto you, and ye shall be my sons and daughters, saith the Lord Almighty." Know that you are now a part of "Abba" Father, your new spiritual family. A spiritual relationship that is eternal and will be so if you stay spiritually connected to Him.

CHAPTER 5

DISORDER

The Culture of the world as we have experienced and visualized is in cruel disorder. The United States of America since I've known has been the one place where many people have wanted to reside. Many years ago, we heard stories of different nationalities and how their parents struggled in foreign lands. How many of them came here to live because of the benefits from our government. Not only that, but people were able to live in our country, at one time promoted justice, equality and civil order.

But now, even in this 20th century, things have taken a turn for the worse. The societal norms, morality and values have decayed so much so that our own political arena has chosen to remove the moral standards and righteous Godly beliefs. The beliefs at one time were followed respectively and there was a prominent fear of God. Yes! all and a small margin have chosen to followed these beliefs. Someway people have turned away from these standards of truth. The scripture in Isaiah 59:14 clearly tells us our sins, "And judgment is turned away backward, and justice standeth afar of; for truth is fallen in the street, and equity cannot enter."

It leaves us with a questions, What happened to us? Why did we choose to leave the very righteous standards that blessed our home and our families.

Why would two glorious humans rebel and reject God's beautiful paradise Eden. The answer is because one woman listened to liars of the enemy, Satan. Our world that is never ending a sinful catastrophe into deadly judgment.

The word "disorder" is defined as:

1. Want of order or regular disposition; lack of arrangement; confusion; disarray; as, the troops were thrown into disorder; the papers are in disorder.

2. (n.) Neglect of order or system; irregularity.

3. (n.) Breach of public order; disturbance of the peace of society; tumult.

4. (n.) Disturbance of the functions of the animal economy of the soul; sickness; derangement.

5. (v. t.) To disturb the order of; to derange or disarrange; to throw into confusion; to confuse.

6. (v. t.) To disturb or interrupt the regular and natural functions of (either body or mind); to produce sickness or indisposition in; to discompose; to derange; as, to disorder the head or stomach.

7. (v. t.) To depose from holy orders.

8. The increase in criminal acts and total disorder in the family order

All of these are good definitions, but the one definition that stands out is "To depose from holy orders." God's one holy order to his two humans, Adam and Eve was to not eat of the tree of knowledge of good and evil. The message of the gospel proclaims the death, burial, and resurrection of our Lord Jesus Christ. It is the inspired word of God and able to saved humanity, proclaiming the message of repentance. In II Timothy 3:16 "All scripture is given by inspiration of God, and is profitable for doctrine, for reproof, for correction, for instruction in righteousness." Any problem or situation in this fallen world can be addressed by the doctrines of the Bible. Just a few to mention these doctrines, are salvation, Holy Spirit, man, church, the last days and mostly how to live holy and following God's commands. Our Holy Bible commands and admonish believers to live by certain beliefs.

These beliefs are foundational standards and principles that were given to God's 40 holy men as they were penned in his 66 books of the Bible. This fallen world has chosen to subvert from obeying and living by these commanded beliefs, doctrines, and principles of Christianity.

Let us discuss and review the church of Corinth. There are some lessons to be learned from this church, in Corinth. Within this church there was a stream of divisions in all areas of their ministry. Paul, the apostle, began penning his letter with a thoughtful consideration to remedy the confused situation by giving rebuke, correction and instruction. This church was established in the city that was infested with paganism. The city of Corinth was centered around materialism and moral corruption. The people of this church refused to follow certain doctrines and biblical principles. There was no limit to the sinful plagues in this church atmosphere.

Paul was summoned to address disorderly complaints that caused sinful behavior. Paul's letter in detail pointed to specific disorders, divisions that polluted the mindsets of the church. These disorders were related to morality problems, disputes of certain teachings, appropriate freedoms for believers, worship, monetary actions, and importance of resurrection matters. Paul admonished the Corinthian church with thanksgiving and the many blessings of God's grace.

Paul's heart was filled with dire concern that the Corinthian church dedicate itself to a closer fellowship in Jesus. In I Corinthians 1:9 He writes "God is faithful, by whom ye were called unto the fellowship of his Son Jesus Christ our Lord." The bottom line here is that Jesus called our churches to have true fellowship.

Paul's appeal for the return to oneness and leaving disorder and confusion was stressed strongly in this verse. In I Corinthians 1:10 "Now I beseech you, brethren, by the name of our Lord Jesus Christ, that ye all speak the same thing, and that there be no divisions among you; but that ye be perfectly joined together in the same mind and in the same judgment."

Paul's urgent request was for them to follow a more orderly mindset, being perfectly joined together in the same judgment.

Paul's assignment was to help the Corinthian church to repent and turn back to following his commandments, that of the truth of Jesus principles, exercising spiritual purity and allowing the power of the Holy Ghost to prevail.

The true church of God, His bride of Christ should be displaying righteousness as he commanded. Ephesians 5:27 "That he might present it to himself a glorious church, not having spot, or wrinkle, or any such thing; but that it should be holy and without blemish."

When the congregants take the precious word of God and apply it to their spiritual life, they desire to walk in the Holy Spirit and allow God's word to cleanse them from sinful inclinations. Paul's message was to alert everyone to perfect their spiritual life. In Colossians 1:28 "Whom we preach, warning every man, and teaching every man in all wisdom; that we may present every man perfect in Christ Jesus:" Let's look at the meaning of "perfect." In Hebrew it is translated "tamin" and means whole, sound, healthy having integrity. It tells us in Matthew 5:48 "Be ye therefore perfect, even as your Father which is in heaven is perfect." Our leaders are placed in ministry to make sure that we are fed spiritual truths that relate to the doctrines and principles of the faith. They are also given the task to present us to God. In Hebrews 13:17 "Obey them that have the rule over you and submit yourselves: for they watch for your souls, as they that must give account, that they may do it with joy, and not with grief: for that is unprofitable for you." We have learned that we must obey, we must follow, and we must pursue holiness. When we are filled with the Holy Spirit, it helps us, the spirit teaches us how to be holy in this evil world. Holiness is a beauty virtue, because it brings fellowship with God, and helps us to be righteous. Being holy helps us to be separated for his service, set apart for love, and worship toward God. The more we grow spiritually in him, the more we become dedicated and desire to please him in all our ways as we change.

Our ultimate spiritual endeavor is to not turn toward sin, yet if we do, we can confess, and God is faithful to forgive us as declared in (I John1:9) God's chosen leaders are anointed to preach the word of God with conviction and persuasion. Romans 6:1-2 "What shall we say then? Shall we continue in sin, that grace may abound?" Herein lays the answer, verse (2) God forbid, How shall we, that are dead to sin, live any longer therein? We each have a choice in the matter of how we will live here on this earth. The bad choice is eternal death, and the good choice is abundant life. in John 3:20 "For everyone that doeth evil hateth the light, neither cometh to the light, lest his deeds should be reproved."

When you turn away from God and follow the path of sin, you open yourself to a life of destruction, you leave his protection and mostly you allow evil to become your partner. As foretold in the Bible, Jesus spoke a future warning as a sign to stay watchful and alert. Jesus stressed that the spirit of deception would be prevalent. In Matthew 24:4-6 "Take heed that no man deceive you, For many shall come in my name, saying, I am Christ; and shall deceive many. And ye shall hear of wars and rumors of wars: see that ye be not troubled; for all these things must come to pass, but the end is not yet." The signs of the last days are in II Timothy 3:1-3 "This know also, that in the last days perilous times shall come.

For men shall be lovers of their own selves, covetous, boasters, proud, blasphemers, disobedient to parents, unthankful, unholy, Without natural affection, trucebreakers, false accusers, incontinent, fierce, despisers of those that are good." The standards of right and wrong are no more in our day and age, people, children, whomever have pursued the path of evil as if it was a daily norm. It seems like to me as it was in the days of Israel in Judges 21:25 "In those days there was no king in Israel; everyone did what was right in his own eyes." Yes! on the other hand, we have leaders in our government, but the laws of the land are not upheld and have become perverse and interpreted in wrong opinions. We need order in our government, in our schools, our businesses, families and individual lives. We can conclude from sharing the above scriptures that this world we live in is filled with wickedness and confusion. We are living on dangerous ground surrounded by risky situations and hazardous times. In James 3:16 "For where envying and strife is, there is confusion and every evil work." We need to return to God, meaning the only way we can get our homes right, our families back to praying and having devotions is to start individually. To get our spiritual house in order, we need to change the way we live, how we cherish our relationships, we need to change our mindset and mostly establish a spiritual relationship with God.

Below, this is just my exhibit of what I believe should be our standard of righteousness. As each believer continues to draw closer to God, He will guide you, teach you and counsel you through the Holy Ghost, how to maintain a lifestyle of holiness.

MODEL OF DIVINE ORDER

DISORDER → **DIVINE ORDER**
CRUCIFY FLESH / FEARING GOD
CARNAL MINDSET / MAINTAINING HOLINESS
REBELLION / AGAPE LOVE
DISOBEDIENCE / OBEY HIS WORD

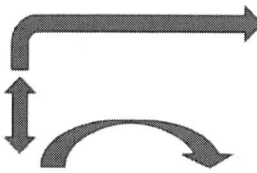

ORDERLY PRACTICES
REPENTANCE/SALVATION
YOUR PRAYER MINISTRY
APPLICATION OF HIS WORD
STUDYING HIS WORD

We will experience blessing in our lives, which will allow us to reach new levels of knowledge and teach wisdom of God. The favor and glory of God will be prominent among our assemblies because we endeavor to keep the oneness mindset that offsets confusion. I enjoyed this verse of scripture because it speaks truth Psalm 119:133 "Order my steps in thy word: and let not any iniquity have dominion over me"

Another Translation in NIV - "Direct my footsteps according to your word; let no sin rule over me." As we allow our God to direct us, we protect our self from the evils of sin.

It will take much prayer and much spiritual warfare to align our steps and walk in his word. We stop the sin nature from being the prominent ruler of our spiritual life. When we do this persistently, we allow God's righteousness to prevail, showing forth spiritual integrity. You will have to diligently speak to your mind, heart and command them to submit to God, helping you to stay in the straight and narrow way. Proverbs 3:5-6 "Trust in the LORD with all your heart; and lean not on your own understanding; in all your ways submit to him, and he will make your paths straight."

Our ways are not God's ways, because God has the correct path for us to follow. Isaiah 55:8 "For my thoughts are not your thoughts, neither are your ways my ways, saith the Lord." We must sincerely and boldly put our trust in God as we submit to his divine order it brings clarity and spiritual direction. Serving God and living for God in this fallen world will require us surrendering to his wisdom. Yes! we will question his order, but in the end know that you will receive peace and spiritual prosperity. When we individually read his word, apply it to our lives and begin to live out his word. The things of the past, the temporal pleasures will be insignificant, because now we have chosen to connect to a God that will change your sin nature to God's nature. You will begin to display the virtues of righteousness, living a sanctified and consecrated life for his glory. No more, Why did I act that way? Why did I say those evil words? Why did I commit that evil act?

You know why, because you have come to realize that your ways are not pleasing to God. You are confessing your short comings and your sins so that your will can align with God's will. You are diligently endeavoring to maintain your spiritual progress in Christ, so that he will be glorified in you. You become convicted of your conscience to turn from something or some habit of sin. Convince and commit yourself to receive the power and fire of His Holy Spirit to lead you, to guide you and to counsel you. You were born with sin nature with the will to commit all kinds of evil. God wants to set you free, to remove the curse, To redeem you to bring you back to the original order. When God finishes molding you, shaping you into the glorious person he wants you to be, you will step back and say why did I take so long to surrender to his will. God's promise is embedded in this precious word in Jude 24-25 "Now to him who is able to keep you from falling, and to present you faultless before the presence of His glory with exceeding joy. To the only wise God our Savior, be glory and majesty, dominion and power, both now and forever". Amen.

"Experience His Divine Order now in this life and forever"

CHAPTER 6

GOD'S PURPOSE

God's purpose is to redeem humanity and to bring them back to the original order of emanating God's image and his glory. God's desire is that humanity would accept abundant life through his Son Jesus Christ. Proverbs 19:21 notes in the heart of a man "There are many devices in a man's heart; nevertheless the counsel of the Lord, that shall stand."

God's Order of Kingdom Purpose

- Worship

- Fellowship

- Discipleship

- Ministry

- Evangelism

As these Kingdom purposes prevail God's Kingdom of light will grow to such a degree that everyone will be in total union with returning back to His Divine Order. There will be unity in the Spirit as urged in Ephesians 4:3 "Endeavoring to keep the unity of the Spirit in the bond of peace".

In the beginning when God made man His purpose for them was to be fruitful, and multiply, and replenish the earth, and subdue it; and have dominion over the elements of nature. Adam was given one commandment to follow, and he refused because of the enemy's deception through his wife, Eve. This brought on eternal separation from God, which later brought on confusion and chaos for them, henceforth for individuals, families, and nations. Throughout the 66 books of the Holy Bible God's will and purpose is for humanity to be saved so that they would not endure his judgment and wrath.

God love's for humanity was consistent, despite repeated sin, God's judgment was applied, Yet he will not tolerate sin. as a result of one's disobedience and rejection of the gospel. God commissioned his apostles to spread the gospel message. In the Roman era, the Pharisees and Sadducees cause chaos and division amongst the community of believers. The church was persecuted by rejecters for such an enormous growth of Christian believers. Some of the disciples in this era fell away from the faith. Despite this dilemma. God's resolute apostles, endured chastening, persecution and even were marked for execution.

His faithful and resolute leaders chose to continue preaching regardless of the disregard and denial of Jews and Gentiles accepting Jesus as Messiah. Yet, even amid rejection of the message, souls were being baptized and filled with the Holy Spirit. God's message was outlined by holy men who were inspired to write by the Holy Spirit. The word "inspired" translated in Greek "theopneustos" comes from two Greek words "theos" meaning God and "pneô" meaning to "breathe," Thus inspired means "God-breathed." All the holy scriptures are authoritative and is without doubt able to stand against false doctrines and ungodly opinions. All of the scriptures were preserved centuries ago and translated to present a strong foundational message. These scriptures provide the plan of salvation, how to stay saved, how to be delivered and how to be healed. God also inspired his holy men to give instruction in righteousness. II Timothy 3:16 "All scripture is given by inspiration of God, and is profitable for doctrine, for reproof, for correction, for instruction in righteousness." God wants his holy believers to live a holy life. When God spoke prophetic words recorded in the Old Testament, he declared the church's future and his second coming for the world, he already knew centuries beforehand what the outcome and intentions of humanity. Jesus in his ministry poured out from his very soul sermons on the mount, to teach those who were hungry for understanding and truth.

Jesus lived by example of love, compassion, and empathy for those who were broken, oppressed, diseased and hurt. Jesus way and idea of order was for his called and chosen disciples to carry the gospel message to humanity over the entire world. Jesus lived by example and taught messages that astonished his hearers. In Matthew 13:54 "And when he was come into his own country, he taught them in their synagogue, insomuch that they were astonished, and said, Whence hath this man this wisdom, and these mighty works?" Jesus message caused his rejecters to be offended because the words that he spoke pricked their hearts and conscience. They felt guilty to change their religious mindset. The ultimate purpose in his message was that the light of the glorious gospel would draw souls for the future kingdom.

When one becomes a believer, we are committing to God's ways, learning his wisdom, experiencing his love, and trusting his sovereignty. Yet, for those who desire to remain steadfast in their spiritual walk, they will encounter a struggle with the flesh and the spirit. The enemy knows that he has lost a soul and will try every shrewd plan and scheme to turn that soul back to his kingdom of darkness.

Without order, there is confusion. God is not a God of disorder (confusion), but of peace. God's purpose of order in his kingdom of light requires, the church his body of believers to practice fellowship in unity and follow love amongst all believers.

God's purpose for us is to be transformed in our character. As we are being transformed we reflect His image and his virtues. God's purpose is to deposit essential orders in the life of each believer, with the power of the Holy Spirit. He can succeed bringing forth fruits of his righteousness and a spiritual menagerie of blessings. In Ephesians 1:3-6 "Blessed be the God and Father of our Lord Jesus Christ, who has blessed us with all spiritual blessings in the heavenly places in Christ: according as he hath chosen us in him before the foundation of the world, that we should be holy and without blame before him. in love: having predestinated us unto the adoption of children by Jesus Christ to himself, according to the good pleasure of his will, To the praise of the glory of his grace, wherein he hath made us accepted in the beloved."

Purpose of God's Blessings

1. Seated in heavenly places

2. Chosen in Him

2. Be Holy and Blameless

4. In His Love

5. Predestinated

6. Adopted Children

7. Good Pleasure of His will

8. Praise and Glory of His Grace.

God has a remedy from our past a plan outlined for our soul salvation Ephesians 2:1-6 "And you hath he quickened, who were dead in trespasses and sins; Wherein in time past ye walked according to the course of this world, according to the prince of the power of the air, the spirit that now worketh in the children of disobedience:" Among whom also we all had our conversation in times past in the lusts of our flesh, fulfilling the desires of the flesh and of the mind; and were by nature the children of wrath, even as others. But God, who is rich in mercy, for his great love wherewith he loved us, Even when we were dead in sins, hath quickened us together with Christ, (by grace ye are saved;) and hath raised us up together, and made us sit together in heavenly places in Christ Jesus:"

The moment you desire to be obedient to his will and purpose, God begins the work of righteousness that of "quickening". That spiritual 'quickening" means to "revive or make alive," you were spiritual dead in trespasses and sins. meaning his order (new birth) in your life provided spiritual restoration back to God's original design for your life. It is in this spiritual restoration that we say "Yes" inviting the Holy Spirit to reside on the inside of our inner man, your spirit. When you align your life with His will, and become saved, you are becoming a candidate for his good works In Ephesians 2:10 "For we are his workmanship, created in Christ Jesus unto good works, which God hath before ordained that we should walk in them." You are no longer under judgment; you want to experience all the benefits of your spiritual blessings now and forever. In Ephesians 3:11 "According to the eternal purpose which he purposed in Christ Jesus our Lord:" Every God given promise and purpose is based on the foundation of Christ Jesus our Lord. Stand on the true foundation, firmly while you follow God's directives. Each step that you take will move you closer to your heavenly destination. Trust him and genuinely love him. He has good things in store for you. God has a new kingdom and a new heaven right now being prepared for his "ecclesia" His "church" the Bride of Christ.

When we get to heaven, we will be celebrating His glory forever praising and magnifying God.

In this present world God has called us to be his holy believers standing on the foundation of Jesus Christ. As declared in I Peter2:5 "Ye also, as lively stones, are built up a spiritual house, an holy priesthood, to offer up spiritual sacrifices, acceptable to God by Jesus Christ"

Don't you desire to be filled with his glory, His righteousness, His fire? his "living stones" that of a spiritual house with the sole purpose offering up spiritual sacrifices to God. Decide to put away the cares of the world, the vices of the world that hold you in bondage, not allowing God's freedom to avail in your life. Desire to seek his word, his principles, and doctrines so that you can have a roadmap of being separated and consecrated for his glory. That is God's good pleasure for you to give you the kingdom. When you strive in this order you bring peace and joy to your soul.

The author Paul, the apostle penned a key verse for the assembly of believers to strive to maintain orderly ministry and remain in a spirit of harmony. In I Corinthians 14:40 "Let all things be done decently and in order." No matter what ministry that God choses you for, whether praise and worship, Sunday school, serving other believers, or prayer ministry do so in a spirit of orderliness. As we do this, we maintain decency in our churches to be harmonious amongst our brothers and sisters in Christ.

Our fallen world includes people doing things that are contrary to the standards of biblical truth and morality. Their one and only sinful purpose is to follow the carnal desires of the flesh. This is not an acceptable will for humanity, His will in the writings of the New Testament reinforces an idea of order that produces peace and unity.

Teaching us to order our exterior life and producing a reflection of our interior lives. He speaks of prioritizing love for God and our neighbor, obedience to doing his word and applying it to our lives, highlighting the importance of humility and servant hood. If His church, the future Bride of Christ is portraying righteousness, holiness and consecration there will be fruits of orderliness. Each believer pursuing order in their own lives, their families, home, world, and nation.

CHAPTER 7

GOD'S GLORY

Our God's glory is displayed throughout his creation in Genesis 2 his creative works. God expresses his glory through his redemptive acts. God's people can experience his glory when we have a relationship with God, we should be experiencing change, taking on the image of our God. II Corinthians 3:18 "But we all, with open face beholding as in a glass the glory of the Lord, are changed into the same image from glory to glory, even as by the Spirit of the Lord."

This glory involves us taking time in his presence, or when we study his word and abide in his word, we learn about the truth of his glory. The more we take time to meditate and study his word we allow order in our life; the holy word begins to transform us working through the power of the Holy Spirit. When God wants an ordered and unified body of believers offering up praises and worship to him, he is being glorified. Hallelujah!

What is glory? I am glad you asked, it is the visible manifestation of the presence and power of God. It is defined in Hebrew as "kabod" in Greek "doxa," it is God's person, presence, his redemptive works.

When I wake up in the morning the first thing, I do is draw back the curtains and open the blinds. It is a brand-new day and I look up toward the sky, the heavens and marvel at God's creation. I thank God for a brand-new day of life. All of God's creation is declaring his glory. (Psalms 19:1) The glory crown is significant because it all started in the beginning when God made man, God wants us to strive to receive more of his glory in degrees and levels. How magnificent is God in that when he made man, he crowned him with glory and honor. Psalm 8:5 "For thou hast made him a little lower than the angels, and hast crowned him with glory and honor." God's glory is testifying and declaring his creation in the heavens and the firmament, as well as in all of his creation in Genesis 2nd chapter. The gospel writer's portray Christ's glory explaining his total person. Matthew gave us Christ as the Jesus, the Messianic King, Mark gave us Jesus the Servant Son, Luke gave us Jesus, the Savior and John gave us Jesus, the Son of God.

In the book of Exodus. God's glorified servant "Moses "experienced the glory. He had to put a veil over his face because of the glory of God. Exodus 34:33 "And till Moses had done speaking with them, he put a veil on his face." What was profound to me was Moses spent 40 days and forty nights, talking with God. Amazing! Hallelujah! (Exodus 34:28) Our countenance and character should be a resemblance of his image. His glory should be covering us and lightning up our very face. I must share this glory experience.

I was at Wal-Mart one Sunday morning picking up photos, and when I faced the clerk, he kept staring at me, he said "Something about you" you are different, I wondered what I did, and then it dawned on me that the enemy was vexed at the glory and the anointing on my life. The clerk told me "take your photos" and go you do not owe us anything," This I will never forget. When we seriously consecrate and dedicate ourselves to the ministry and work of God, his glory is deposited on us. Our lives, therefore, should reflect this divine mandate, indicating the importance of aligning with God's order, his light in us emanates in a dark and evil world. God is being glorified when we walk in his divine order. God is pleased and delighted when we are obedient. In Psalms 37:23 "The steps of a good man are ordered by the LORD: and he delighted in his way." There are so many other ways God's glory is revealed.

Glory Revealed

- In his Incarnation

- His birth

- His transfiguration

- Suffering and Crucifixion

- His Resurrection

- His Ascension

- Holy Spirit (Pentecost)

There was an incident in I Samuel 4:21 where the glory of God departed and the birth of a child was named "Ichabod," because the Ark of the Covenant had been captured by the nation of Israel's enemy, the Philistines. What has been captured in your life? Are wrapped up in darkness? Has sin converged on your mind, your emotions, or your being? Do you feel like God has left you?

Examine yourself and inspect your spiritual life and determine where you are in God, this is the time to reorder your life, so that you can come back to God. Do you need to repent and cry out of your soul and say, "Lord restore me back to your presence, renew my relationship with you" God is right there waiting for your "Yes." God wants you to experience his glory, his favor and all his mercy. God wants to be our shield and the lifter up of our heads. When we totally surrender, we are no longer under the rule of bondages and darkness. God wants us to illuminate his glory in our demeanor; it is changing us for his glorification.

God gives us power, cover us with his glory and anoints us so that we can bind evil spirits and principality and command them to leave our presence.

When you participate in the baptism of the Holy Spirit you are ordering a new life in Christ. The Holy Ghost power helps you to conquer, destroy, and nullify the works of Satan. Even when we are faced with difficult trials, persecutions and storms in our life, God has given us all the spiritual tools we need to fight this fight of faith. Use your divine order of authority to tread on serpents and all the power of the enemy. Pray in the Holy Ghost until you receive a release in the spirit and answers in your dilemmas. Use the word of God by decreeing and declaring it over your circumstances.

Pray a prayer and ask God to help you walk in the majesty, and the brilliance and fullness of his glory. In Romans 8:18 "For I reckon that the sufferings of this present time are not worthy to be compared with the glory which shall be revealed in us."

Your future is wrapped around His Glory.

CHAPTER 8

NOAH- GOD'S ENGINEER

There are also men recorded in the Old Testament Bible that said "Yes" to God's will. These were just ordinary men whom God called and chose to complete specific assignments. Let us begin with Noah. Noah was a faithful preacher and skilled engineer. Noah's name meant "rest or repose." Noah totally rested in the peace of God. Noah believed that no matter how long his task he would finish it. Noah found grace that is God's "favor" he was a just man, perfect in his generation and he walked with God. When we submit to God's will, ask the God of your salvation to give you determination and diligence to follow His ordered steps. Even though there was corruption, violence and evil in his day, Noah was steadfast "ordered" in his character. In Genesis 6:11-12 "The earth also was corrupt before God, and the earth was filled with violence. And God looked upon the earth, and behold, it was corrupt; for all flesh had corrupted his way upon the earth." People all around him were evil continually. There was no goodness too be found in their souls. God found one man Noah who was conscious of God and lived an orderly life. God ordered Noah's steps, he gave him the blueprint for the massive building of the ark and the finality of his ordered task was secured with the Noahic Covenant.

In Genesis 6:18 "But with thee will I establish my covenant; and thou shalt come into the ark, thou, and thy sons, and thy wife, and thy sons' wives with thee." Noah was troubled by all the chaos and confusion and evil around him, but Noah refused to divert from walking with his God. God seriously kept Noah on track with his assignment. In Hebrews 11:7 "By faith Noah, being warned of God of things not seen as yet, moved with fear, prepared an ark to the saving of his house; by the which he condemned the world, and became heir of the righteousness which is by faith." In Matthew 24:37-39 "But as the days of Noah were, so shall also the coming of the Son of man be. For as in the days that were before the food they were eating and drinking, marrying and giving in marriage, until the day that Noah entered into the ark. And knew not until the food came, and took them all away; so, shall also the coming of the Son of man be." It was not recorded in this story of Noah, but I do believe that the people in his era were mocking him, laughing at him and calling him names. Noah's call to build the Ark was 120 years. Noah's dedication to God resulted in his holiness being a light in a sinful world. God founded Noah and commended him because of his righteous character.

When you consciously live holy, and are obedient to God, he will pick you for some awesome and extraordinary charge.

But, when you become a part of the world system and blend in with their evil ways, it only leads to downward destruction and eternal judgment. Preventing you from missing godly opportunities that would have benefited you spiritually from receiving God's eternal blessing.

CHAPTER 9

MAN OF FAITH ABRAHAM (ABRAM)

Abraham exemplified strong and enduring faith. There were other notable men who walked with God, that of Enoch, Daniel and Job, these faithful servants lived among evil circumstances, but God saw fit to deliver them. (Ezekiel 14:14). God instructed Abraham to leave Canaan his father's house. God also said, "I will show you the land I have for you." Abraham was 75 years old when he left Canaan, an unfamiliar place with his servants and wife. God had a divine order for Abraham. When God gives a specific order, walk by faith, and put away doubt and except the promise not in unbelief. Paul admonished us with this encouragement of faith Roman 4:20-22 "He staggered not at the promise of God through unbelief; but was strong in faith, giving glory to God;" And being fully persuaded that, what he had promised, he was able also to perform." And therefore, it was imputed to him for righteousness." Abram was given credit on record for his faith in God.

Abraham was a man of God who walks steadily in his faith, meaning he was unwavering, he possessed strong faith. Abraham's was fully persuaded that the God he served and prayed to was skillful, all knowing to fulfill his promise.

This is the kind of faith we need, when God orders you to move into new arenas, trusting in your God. Do not be afraid! Do what Abraham did, like our Bishop Wallace says "Go to sleep" give it to our God. Guess what, Abraham had a vision in Genesis 15:1-2 "After these things the word of the Lord came unto Abram in a vision, saying, Fear not, Abram: I am thy shield and thy exceeding great reward." And Abram said, Lord God, what wilt thou give me, seeing I go childless, and the steward of my house is this Eliezer of Damascus." God read the table of Abraham's heart, "Don't fear" meaning "I got your back Abraham, I AM your "Jehovah Jireh" your Provider. Abraham, I will protect you from all harm. Meditate on this "I AM" your exceeding great reward. Know that your faith is currency in the realm of asking, seeking, and finding. Yes! Abraham questioned his God and God comforted his heart that he had more than a son to give him, but he had a whole strip of nations and lands for his possession.

Abraham was taught great patience, he desired to have a son, so that all he possessed would be inherited by him. Abraham hearkened to the voice of his wife In Genesis 16:3 "And Sara Abram's wife took Hagar her maid the Egyptian, after Abram had dwelt ten years in the land of Canaan and gave her to her husband Abram to be his wife." Yet, the insistence of his wife, Abraham took his maid Hagar, his wife and had a son "Ishmael."

This one incident during his life deviated Abraham from his faith walk causing many problems in the future for many nations. Obedience often leads to blessings, while disobedience can result in turmoil. Abraham was eighty-six years old when his handmaid conceived their son "Ishmael."

In Genesis 17:1 The Lord God appeared unto Abraham 'And when Abram was ninety years old and nine, the Lord appeared to Abram, and said unto him, I am the Almighty God: walk before me and be thou perfect." God established the Abrahamic Covenant with him that was sign and a token of being everlasting.

In Genesis 17:4 "As for me, behold my covenant is with thee, and thou shalt be a father of many nations. "In Genesis 17:5 "Neither shall thy name any more be called Abram, but thy name shall be Abraham; for a father of many nations have I made thee." His name was changed from Abram to "Abraham" meaning "exalted father." In Genesis 17:21 "But my covenant will I establish with Isaac, which Sarah shall bear unto thee this set time in the next year." Now when Abraham was 100 years old, God talked to Abraham again and promised him he would have a son. In (Genesis 17:17) "Then Abraham fell upon his face, and laughed, and said in his heart, Shall a child be born unto him that is an hundred years old? And shall Sarah, that is ninety years old, bear?

Abraham laughed, I could imagine him rolling in the dust and repeatedly laughing, "Who me at my age, to have a son."

Abraham should have realized that his lighthearted chuckle was a sign of unbelief. Abraham did not realize that this one great order would change his family and the nation of Israel. This was Abraham's true test of faith in the God. God responded Genesis 18:14 "Is anything too hard for the Lord? At the time appointed I will return unto thee, according to the time of life, and Sarah shall have a son." The order of God's promise was fulfilled because Abraham had his son "Isaac" at the set year as his God had spoken. Who would have thought that this word of promise would take over thirty years. It is interesting from this lengthy story that the lesson learned is to be patient. God will stick true to his word, unequivocally what he spoke, because he does not liar, he is immutable, meaning he does not change his mind. When he gives you an order trust me it will happen. In Numbers 23:19 "God is not a man, that he should lie; neither the son of man, that he should repent: hath he said, and shall he not do it? Or hath he spoken, and shall he not make it good? Herein is a divine declaration In Malachi 3:6 "For I am the Lord, I change not; therefore, ye sons of Jacob are not consumed."

God is complete and orderly in giving truth, when he speaks his word it can stand, because his man and women were examples because they lived by the holy word of God. When you allow your heart to hear truth, you are declaring to God that you are not governed by your intellect, or you own understanding.

You submit to God so that your path and your relationship is straight.

In Proverbs 3:5-6 "Trust in the LORD with all thine heart; and lean not unto thine own understanding." In all thy ways acknowledge him, and he shall direct thy paths."

In closing its spiritually important that God can say "Put your name here" I know" - I liked this Genesis 18:19 "For I know him, that he will command his children and his household after him, and they shall keep the way of the Lord, to do justice and judgment; that the Lord may bring upon Abraham that which he hath spoken of him." God already knew in his all-knowing ways because he is omniscient, that his servant Abraham would not fail him. God's divine order for Abraham was futuristic as promised. Ask yourself these questions, Are you working toward pleasing God in all your ways? Are you submitting, surrendering your mind, your heart so that the orders he prophetically speaks for you can manifest? It is up to your faith and your total obedience to his will for your life. When God begins the process of orderliness he sees it through fruition.

No matter what challenges life brings you, God always has a plan and purpose far greater than your imagination. You may have experienced a death of a loved one, not received the promotion you expected or in a cycle of depression. You may be experiencing oppression, tormenting pain every day, but realize when you say "Yes' God is pleased with your commitment and affirmation. God hears your plea and your supplication; he knows right where you are. God knows just what you need, he has the perfect direction, the right destiny, and clear instructions for you to follow. But know this, your "Yes" is the answer to your breakthrough, your "Yes" opens the doors to access all his promises. Your "Yes" accompanied by your mustard seed of faith, will authorize you to move the mountains of life and command them to be cast into the sea. You must hold onto to your "Yes" it has eternal ramifications. Do not be like Esau and exchange it for a mere bowl of beans. Your "yes" has value in God's eyes. Hebrews 10:23 Let us hold fast the profession of our faith without wavering: (for he is faithful the promised.

CHAPTER 10

Paul God's Spokesman

Paul's birth was recorded in A.D. 6 which took place in Rome, in the city of Tarsus in Cilicia (Turkey) according Acts 21:39. Paul's education and facets of Judaism was schooled under prominent leaders, Acts 22:3 "I am verily a man which am a Jew, born in Tarsus, a city in Cilicia, yet brought up in this city at the feet of Gamaliel, and taught according to the perfect manner of the law of the fathers, and was zealous toward God, as ye all are this day." Paul also spoke Greek and Hebrew languages. His name "Saul" was taken from the name of the Old Testament king Saul as history recorded. Paul was such that he was affluent in a number languages and a traveler to many regions was able to relate to the many cultures that he encountered. Paul's hatred of Christianity begin in A.D. 30-33 persecuting followers of Jesus in the way.

Regardless of one's past, God always choses and call individuals with the worst background of character and personality to place in positions of exception in the ministry. Then on the other hand he chooses those individuals who their peers may assume are unlearned and ignorant.

Usually when a government official is nominated for a position they are questioned before a panel of their peers, undergoing issues concerning their family life, finances, standard beliefs, and character. When it is all over, they may be selected or denied for their nomination. But our God, is compassionate, forgiving and looks at the heart of the individual, long before the outcome of his calling on their life. God is not like man, unforgiving, holding on to past offenses or evil acts. When God orders your steps, he has a specific exceptional purpose in mind. Yet, God's power and the Holy Ghost can work through you producing miracles, signs, and wonders. In Acts 4:13 "Now when they saw the boldness of Peter and John, and perceived that they were unlearned and ignorant men, they marveled; and they took knowledge of them, that they had been with Jesus." From this verse we learn that no matter what the world thinks of you, no matter what your peers know about you, God can work a transformation order in your life. God can give you boldness, God can give you self- confidence and the spiritual ability to preach, teach or sing or minister for his glorification. God wants a willing vessel so that his gospel message can be declared to those who have no inkling of the majesty and power of God.

When the world see's God working in you, they will truly marvel. When God gives you orders it may come through your prayer time, it may come through a prophetic word from a prophet or leader, it can come through a dream or a vision.

God will use whatever means necessary to fulfill his divine will. When you know you are ready for a change in your spiritual life, know that this is God's precise timing and call on your life.

God already knew the wicked steps that Paul was going to take, Acts 8:3 "As for Saul, he made havoc of the church, entering into every house, and haling men and women committed them to prison." Saul was a menace to Christianity, yet in our society and had he been in our day he would have been "put on the FBI most wanted list" Saul was a threat because he caused chaos, he caused disorder, and he caused destruction among the very people that God intended to reach with the gospel message. Even, while Saul had consented to the death of Stephen, there was a widespread persecution to the church in Jerusalem.

The execution of his beloved servant "Stephen," Acts 22:20 "And when the blood of thy martyr Stephen was shed, I also was standing by, and consenting unto his death, and kept the raiment of them that slew him." In Acts 8:1 "And Saul was consenting unto his death. And at that time there was a great persecution against the church which was at Jerusalem; and they were all scattered abroad throughout the region of Judea and Samaria, except the apostles."

God's chosen apostles and others were scattered preaching the gospel message, causing many new conversions, and infilling of the Holy Ghost.

I am sure Saul previously known from his great mentor Gamaliel, a Pharisee his teacher of the law, how he warned their opposers that they touch not the apostles. They were teaching in Solomon's court. For he warned them in Acts 5:39 "But if it be of God, ye cannot overthrow it; lest haply ye be found even to fight against God." Saul knew that all his efforts were fruitless against the mighty God. Saul knew his arms were too short to box with God. God changed the whole scenario of chaos and planned to divert the continuance of this man's wicked schemes. It was now time for God's order to change Paul's road of disorder. God had a plan that would teach Saul a lesson that he would never forget. Saul thought that his plan was unstoppable, he desired a number of adults to snatch and imprison. Saul arrived at the high priest and desired letters to go to Damascus to the synagogues, to bring anyone in the "way," of Jesus Christ, he would take them bound to Jerusalem. Paul encountered his life changing conversion and conversation with God on the way to Damascus. (Acts 9:1-2) Saul was madly enrooted to destroy the people of God, whether he was on a horse in on a chariot, that the light was so powerful that he fell to the ground on his journey. In Acts 9:3-4,6 "And as he journeyed, he came near Damascus: and suddenly there shined round about him a light from heaven:" And he fell to the earth, and heard a voice saying unto him, Saul, Saul, why persecutes thou me?"

"And he trembling and astonished said, Lord, what wilt thou have me to do? And the Lord said unto him, Arise, and go into the city, and it shall be told thee what thou must do." God had a purpose and specific order for Saul in Acts 9:15 "But the Lord said unto him, Go thy way: for he is a chosen vessel unto me, to bear my name before the Gentiles, and kings, and the children of Israel:" Below is our description of the old person "Saul" and the new "Paul" God's servant.

Saul's wicked steps	Paul's Ordered steps
1. Blasphemer	1. A Servant of Christ -Gal 1:10
2. Persecutor	2. Persuader of Christianity-Gentiles
3. Injurious	3. Called by God's grace.
4. Anti-Christian Zeal	4. Filled with the Holy Ghost
5. Pharisee	5. Performed special miracles and wonders
6. Caused havoc churches	6. Gospel by revelation of Jesus Christ. Gal 1:12

Ananias kept Paul at Antioch for one year. Paul left them and stayed in Arabia for three years.

Paul's absence was certified by his own testimony in Galatians 1:11-19 "But I certify you, brethren, that the gospel which was preached of me is not after man."

For I neither received it of man, neither was I taught it, but by the revelation of Jesus Christ." For ye have heard of my conversation in time past in the Jews' religion, how that beyond measure I persecuted the church of God and wasted it:" And profited in the Jews' religion above many my equals in mine own nation, being more exceedingly zealous of the traditions of my fathers." But when it pleased God, who separated me from my mother's womb, and called me by his grace," To reveal his Son in me, that I might preach him among the heathen; immediately I conferred not with flesh and blood:" Neither went I up to Jerusalem to them which were apostles before me; but I went into Arabia, and returned again unto Damascus." Then after three years I went up to Jerusalem to see Peter, and abode with him fifteen days." But other of the apostles saw I none, save James the Lord's brother."

It was then Paul returned to Jerusalem, afterwards, at the church of Antioch, they ministered and fasted with the prophets and teachers. These laid hands on them releasing them by the confirmation of the Holy Ghost to do what God had called them to do. A fantastic miracle took place which involved Paul and Barnabas.

They stopped at Seleucia, Cyprus, and Salamis where a mighty miracle took place.

Acts 13:6-12 And when they had gone through the isle of Paphos, they found a certain sorcerer, a false prophet, a Jew, who name was Barjesus: Which was with the deputy of the country, Sergius Paulus, a prudent man; called Barnabas and Saul, and desired to hear the word of God. (There will be always someone that opposes the work and ministry of God). But Elymas the sorcerer (for so is his name by interpretation) withstood them, seeking to turn away the deputy from the faith. Then Saul, (who also is called Paul,) filled with the Holy Ghost, set his eyes on him, And said, O full of all subtly and all mischief, thou child of the devil, thou enemy of all righteousness, wilt thou not cease to pervert the right ways of the Lord? And now, behold, the hand of the Lord is upon thee, and thou shalt be blind, not seeing the sun for a season.

And immediately there fell on him a mist and a darkness; and he went about seeking someone to lead him by the hand. Then the deputy, when he saw what was done, believed, being astonished at the doctrine of the Lord." After Paul's conversion and his evident revelatory experience at Arabia he was ready to do God's bidding that is preaching to the Gentiles so that they would be introduced into the gospel message. He had learned his lesson well, through God's chastening. Paul had no regrets about what he had left behind.

Philippians 3:8 "Yea doubtless, and I count all things but loss for the excellency of the knowledge of Christ Jesus my Lord: for whom I have suffered the loss of all things, and do count them but dung, that I may win Christ," Paul's choice desire was to be a "Soul Winner of Christ." Paul wanted God's righteousness, living by faith, and following his steps every day. Paul knew that God's divine steps entailed sufferings, persecution and even death, yet his chief goal was to reach forth toward those things that God has planned for me. No matter what you have done in the past, Know that God is forgiving. You may have walked in a bad path, thinking this is ok, this is my way or the highway.

Your own intellect has led you down a road of destruction. Someone may have been repeatedly warning you of danger, but you may have refused to hear. Know that God has a better and wholesome plan of instruction and divine orders for you, if you would accept sound wisdom, things in your life can change.

Make the first step and seek God. When you begin to "seek" this means to be so spiritually absorbed in seeking the kingdom of God and his divine will for your life. When you earnestly and diligently pray for direction God will give you the answers and directives you need to proceed in your spiritual life. Seeking to know God and consecrate yourself from evil and separate from the world's vices will take spiritual warfare through the power of the Holy Ghost.

You can succeed if you rely on the Holy Ghost leading, guiding, and counseling you to become a mighty Christian in your relationship with God. In Matthew 6:33 "Seek ye first the kingdom of God, and his righteousness and all these things will be added unto you."

Yet, Paul, the apostle considered himself to be the least of the named apostles, I Corinthians 15:9 "For I am the least of the apostles, that am not meet to be called an apostle, because I persecuted the church of God." Yet God had for him a magnificent work. Paul felt unworthy of his calling by God. Paul wanted to stay humble, and he constantly reminded himself of his past, though he was forgiven of God. He just went out right and named all his sins and wrong doings.

I Timothy 1:12-15 "And I thank Christ Jesus our Lord, who hath enabled me, for that he counted me faithful, putting me into the ministry;" Who was before a blasphemer, and a persecutor, and injurious: but I obtained mercy, because I did it ignorantly in unbelief." And the grace of our Lord was exceeding abundant with faith and love which is in Christ Jesus." This is a faithful saying, and worthy of all acceptations, that Christ Jesus came into the world to save sinners; of whom am chief."

A good lesson learned from the life of Paul in I Timothy 1:16 "Howbeit for this cause I obtained mercy, that in me first Jesus Christ might shew forth all longsuffering, for a pattern to them which should hereafter believe on him to life everlasting." God extended mercy when he did not deserve it. God shewed Paul his longsuffering and that he would be an example for Christ. I, Paul was a confessed murderer killing Christians. Pauls' life held much self- denial and sacrifice. Paul's excellent teachings to all his churches are cherished forever. We can learn in our church arenas that no matter what persecutions avail our foes need a supernatural outline of divine orders, so that they can change as well. I share this story of Paul with you to help you my new believers and seasoned believers, that no matter where you are in your spiritual life, God has a divine order for you. As Bishop Jefferson encouraged us weeks ago "Step by Step," God was guiding the steps of Paul to save souls that of the Gentile nation. The Jewish nation had outright rejected Jesus, as Messiah, when he was crucified on the cross. Paul's evident birth he knew he was called all along, but it took a series of events to change his erroneous direction and wicked steps. It took God and the revelation of Jesus Christ to ensure that Paul specifically knew the direction he had to follow. Paul was such a great spokesman for Christianity and authored between 13 or 14 epistles and strengthen the churches in his era on several missionary journeys.

CHAPTER 11

ORDER IN PENTECOST

Luke wrote this highly acclaimed book of Acts which bear historical facts of the acts of the Holy Spirit. concerning the early church after Christ's death and ascension, These letters were sent by way of his excellent servant Theophilus. He was a follower of Jesus and a scholar of Paul the apostle. Luke proposed the theme of Acts a ferry narrative and record which is noteworthy "The Triumphant Spread of the gospel through the Power of the Holy Spirit."

The book of Acts records one of the greatest events in the history of the early church, which is "Pentecost." Pentecost refers to the Jewish festival of Shavuot celebrated on the fiftieth day after Passover. Pentecost in Greek (Pentēkosteē) meaning "fiftieth" after the traditional holiday of Easter. This event was witnessed by Jews, and Gentiles and visitors from all over the world who came to Jerusalem for the Feast of Weeks. The writer of the book of Acts, Luke mentions the spread of the gospel from Rome to Jerusalem that of 32 countries, 54 cities, 9 Mediterranean islands, and 95 persons. These territories were covered by Paul, the apostles in (3) missionary journeys.

The summary of Acts "The Triumphant spread of the gospel"

(1) Gentile nations was the highlight of this book,

(2) Holy Spirit in the early church

3) Speaking in tongues throughout the writing

These aspects were proving its necessary to seal the baptism of the Holy Spirit and sound evidence. The book of St. Luke and Acts were both written by Luke, the physician.

Jesus had appeared to the assembly of believers after his resurrection in Acts 1:4 "And being assembled with them, commanded them that they should not depart from Jerusalem, but wait for the promise of the Father, which, saith he, ye have heard of me." This was a commandment from Jesus which could not be overlooked because it held great significance in their obedience, The apostles could not be his witnesses to the world until they were filled and were baptized in the Holy Ghost. The apostles needed the "evidence" or proof that they were filled with the Holy Ghost power speaking in tongues. When you must present your case before the judge and the court system, they are specifically looking for proof, not hearsay.

So, the apostles waited faithfully until the outpouring and endowment of the Holy Ghost power. God had a specific plan and order to follow for this phenomenal event of Pentecost.

The apostles had to be constantly reminded of the importance of prophetic orders. In St. Luke 24:44 "And he said unto them, These are the words which I spake unto you, while I was yet with you, that all things must be fulfilled which were written in the law of Moses, and in the prophets, and in the psalms, concerning, me"

In the book of Acts it describes the historical beginnings of the early church on the day of Pentecost. The early church continued to triumph despite mockers and persecution. They were relentless and bold; They allowed the ministry of the Holy Ghost to work in them. The Lord was able to use his believers to perform signs, wonders, and miracles. This was the proof that drew people to inquire about the evidence of the power.

These supported the important highlights of apostolic doctrine in the book of Acts. As Christ commanded them until He returns.

The disciples had suffered much, witnessed the miraculous power of God's, signs and wonders. They witnessed the resurrection of their Lord and Savior Jesus Christ. Christ did not leave them promise less as he vowed in John 14:17 "for he dwelleth in you and shall be in you." Then when he showed himself to them, he fulfilled his promise in John 20:20-22 "And when he had so said, he shewed unto them his hands and his side.

Then were the disciples glad when they saw the Lord." Then said Jesus to them again, Peace be unto you: as my Father hath sent me, even so send I you." And when he had said this, he breathed on them, and saith unto them, Receive ye the Holy Ghost:" This word breathed in Greek (emphusaō), was also noted in Gen 2:7 as "breathed" in Adam's nostrils.

The writer of John indicates that Jesus was depositing in his disciples life, the very essence of God for their soul and a new transformed person. This wonderful endowment the Holy Spirit was spoken of in Isaiah 32:15 "Until the spirit be poured upon us on high" and as well in Isaiah 59:21 this covenant PROMISE extends to future generations "As for me, this is my covenant with them, saith the Lord; My spirit that is upon thee, and my words which I have put in thy mouth, shall not depart out of thy mouth, nor out of the mouth of thy seed, nor out of the mouth of thy seed's seed, saith the LORD, from henceforth and forever."

The apostles were given a mandate to "go" to teach the gospel message as commissioned, they had to experience the impartation of regeneration; that of a complete transformation of their inner man, both were needed in the baptism of the Holy Spirit on the day of Pentecost. God had a divine design to bring forth a new individual that of a "regenerative believer" to manifest the righteousness of God.

In this plan God wants to choose you, he wants to set you up for an amazing blessing, when you surrender and say "Yes" you become an integral part of the kingdom of God. In I Peter 2:9 "But ye are a chosen generation, a royal priesthood, a holy nation, a peculiar people; that ye should shew forth the praises of him who hath called you out of darkness into his marvelous light:"

Your Spiritual Position when you Say "Yes"

- You are chosen.

- You are royalty.

- You are his priest.

- You belong to a Holy Nation

- You are peculiar.

- You are a praiser

- You are called out of darkness.

- You are in the Kingdom of Light

Your obedience to yield to his voice will begin the process of sanctification, which is separation from the worldly vices for his glory, He has forgiven your sins, and you are called the righteousness of God. Partner with God as you confess your need to have God day by day complete his work of salvation in your life.

On the day of Pentecost there was total oneness in the body of believers and apostles. This spirit of oneness was vital, there was no threat of division, no separatism and no discord. This obedient group of 120 believers all were in unity of one mind, one spirit with the goal of waiting for the promise of Jesus words to manifest. While they were waiting, they continued in one accord praying and lifting supplications unto God. The word "one accord" means "being in agreement with a specific order or conforming."

We do not know how long they waited, but it is apparent that their zeal was so strong that all of them were praying and waiting for the powerful move of God. Paul, the apostle recommended true oneness in I Corinthians 1:10 "Now I beseech you, brethren, by the name of our Lord Jesus Christ, that ye all speak the same thing, and that there be no divisions among you; but that ye be perfectly joined together in the same mind and in the same judgment." I have witnessed oneness in our local assembly where the Holy Ghost fell on individuals, and they were baptized in the Holy Ghost.

Why did this happen? Everyone from babies to adults had one mind, praying, and praising the Lord. When we become unified in our minds and our spirits we block the enemy from prevailing. These 120 believers and apostles were willing to unequivocally say "Yes", and their obedience opened up the windows of heaven.

On the day of Pentecost there are (4) notable signs of the impartation of the Holy Spirit. The first notable evidence was a sound from heaven which indicates an announcement. God was preparing his congregants you are about to experience what you have been waiting for, his outpouring and his infilling of the Holy Ghost. The second sign was a rushing mighty wind denotes movement, the power and presence of God. When God does his work of promise through an element of his creation. God always uses something that is familiar to perform a miracle.

The third sign was an infilling, the 120 people were ready and had emptied out those things that would hinder God's divine deposit. The true Christian will desire to be filled with the knowledge of God, with the fruits of the spirit, filled with joy and most of want to be filled with his Holy Spirit. The fourth sign is the evidence of the possession of Holy Spirit.

That is the evidence of cloven tongues, which is manifested as speaking in tongues, your heavenly language between you and God.

You can have this same experience of Pentecost; you can ask God right now for the Holy Ghost to come into your life. As you are led by the Holy Ghost, he will be your comforter, in time of trouble, he will be your intercessor, teaching you how to pray in the spirit, he will be your advocate, helping you to represent his truth in a murky world. In Romans 8:14 "For as many as are led by the Spirit of God, they are the sons of God."

Look at what wonderful spiritual things the Holy Ghost does for you. In John 16:13 "Howbeit when he, the Spirit of truth, is come, he will guide you into all truth: for he shall not speak of himself; but whatsoever he shall hear, that shall he speak, and he will shew you things to come." No matter what the situation the Holy Ghost comes along side us to pray for our infirmities. Standing by our side as our witness at the throne of grace offering up our supplications unto our God.

In Romans 8:26 "Likewise the Spirit also helpeth our infirmities: for we know not what we should pray for as we ought: but the Spirit itself maketh intercession for us with groaning's which cannot be uttered."

The Pentecost experience did not stop them from speaking in tongues. They needed more than their heavenly language to conquer the spiritual challenges that they would face.

Jesus knew that the mandate and commission to evangelize would be challenging, that is why he gave them most important order for the success of their spiritual life. This order would designate them to be powerful in the spiritual realm and the earthly realm as well. In Acts 1:8 "But ye shall receive power, after that the Holy Ghost is come upon you: and ye shall be witnesses unto me both in Jerusalem, and in all Judaea, and in Samaria, and unto the uttermost part of the earth."

Numerous forms of opposition will come against the believer when they preach the truth of the gospel. There are many false doctrines that are in the world, which have to be refuted by the defense of the scriptures and doctrine. When the word of the living God is preached from a vessel (person) that is holy and living a righteous life, strongholds and demonic forces will be destroyed. We are given the authority to cast out demons, to lay hands on sick bodies, to persuade people to turn to Christ and repent. When you hear the gospel message, it convicts your conscience provoking you to ask yourself a question, What must I do to be saved? The word of God has the answers. If you are seeking and searching how things can change, your answer is in Acts 2:28 "Then Peter said unto them, Repent and be baptized every one of you in the name of Jesus Christ for the remission of sins, and ye shall receive the gift of the Holy Ghost."

God wants you to become one of his believers and to be a part of the kingdom of God, you must accept the gospel message. By repenting from your sins, being godly sorrow and making a 360° spiritual turn around in your life. Having a desire to stop living under the snare and dominion of the enemy Satan and choosing to become a child of God. This repentance must take place in the heart first and then be redirected to your mind to trust in the true and living God. It will take a confession of faith, believing in his word, allowing his Holy Spirit to govern your life. Having a total commitment to love God with all your heart, soul, mind, and strength. Believe that you have the full assurance that God is doing an excellent work in you. Know that he wants to be your Father, in John 1:12 "But as many as received him, to them gave he power to become the sons of God, even to them that believe on his name:" It's important that every church teaching the new birth dual experience that of St. John 3:1-21 the water baptism and baptism of the Holy Ghost, should be experiencing Pentecost daily. God needs serious dedicated believers who boldly and fearlessly declare the gospel message to a fallen world of unbelievers.

CHAPTER 12

ORDER YOUR MIND

In the Garden of Eden Eve was bewitched in her mind, her thoughts were poisoned by lies, deception, mistrust and mostly doubt. Eve let the serpent (enemy) used words to question her relationship with the sovereign God. From the thought of lust to the denial of truth, she ate the fruit. Eve eventually caused humanity to follow a path of sinful disorder that lead to spiritual death and physical death.

The problem with this scenario was disobedience. Eve refused to obey and choose disobedience. Eve did not want to fully obey God's commandment by way of her husband. God had set up a place of joy and peace in the garden of Eden. God had a standard of righteousness for Adam and Eve to follow so that they would not fall. But because of the subtlety of the serpent (enemy) Satan, his evil ways of words, she listened. Eve turned her "Yes" of obedience to the commandment to "No" disobedience.

She refused to consider the sinful implications of her decision. In Genesis 2:16-17 "And the LORD God commanded the man, saying, Of every tree of the garden thou mayest freely eat:" But of the tree of the knowledge of good and evil, thou shalt not eat of it: for in the day that thou eatest thereof thou shalt surely die."

Ask yourself a question? What does God want you to learn from this story?

Just because you are comfortable with your lifestyle, it does not make it ok.

The things that you may be following or participating in may not be giving God glory, only giving you temporary pleasure. You must keep practicing those habits and actions over and over again. When you chose to change your mode of thinking, you will find yourself moving away from those things that were contrary to God and moving into a life of repentance, totally submitting, and confessing your sins, faults, mistakes, shortcomings to God daily.

In Colossians 3:1-2 "If ye then be risen with Christ, seek those things which are above, where Christ sitteth on the right hand of God." Set your affection on things above, not on things on the earth."

This verse of scripture persuades you to seek a new higher level of thinking related to Christ and his principles and doctrine. The word seek in Greek "zēteō" and in our English "to achieve" or "I crave or desire to be more like my God, which is his image of holiness and righteousness.

Early in Jesus ministry men were following him, and Jesus asked them a question "What seek ye?" In St. John 1:38 "Then Jesus turned, and saw them following, and saith unto them, What seek ye?

They said unto him, Rabbi, (which is to say, being interpreted, Master,) where dwellest thou?" I am sure his question took them by surprise, because they were obviously taking notice of his activity, their answer was "Where do you live? there was more behind their inquisitiveness.

Our question to you is Are you seeking God? Do you want him to order your steps? If your answer is "Yes," are you setting your mindset on holy thoughts. Then you have begun a good pattern, you have developed a good habit to put your mind on the things of the Spirit. In Romans 8:5 "For they that are after the flesh do mind the things of the flesh; but they that are after the Spirit the things of the Spirit."

You want to pattern your mind like the mind of Christ thinking on pure thoughts and good thoughts. Philippians 4:8 "Finally, brethren, whatsoever things are true, whatsoever things are honest, whatsoever things are just, whatsoever things are pure, whatsoever things are lovely, whatsoever things are of good report; if there be any virtue, and if there be any praise, think on these things." Are you so serious that you want God to help you to change for the better. You can through the power of the Holy Spirit, He will help you to guard and direct your mind. Even though you think things through using your intellect, your behavior begins in your mind and that is where God's transformation takes place.

It is true read, this is the important spiritual practice for your daily Romans 12:1 "I beseech you therefore, brethren, by the mercies of God, that ye present your bodies a living sacrifice, holy, acceptable unto God, which is your reasonable service. Another crucial point in our lesson is to choose to "set" things in order. In Colossians 3:2 "Set your affection on things above, not on things on the earth." The word "set" in Greek "apeno." Meaning in English to "leave, abandon, vacate" You need to abandon and vacate everything that is not benefiting your spiritual mind. The answer to what we set aside is found in Colossians 3:8-9, God inspired Paul to show us the right thing to do.

Ungodly Mindset (Put off)	Godly Mindset (Put on)
1. Anger	1. Mercies
2. Wrath	2. Kindness
3. Malice	3. Humbleness of mind
4. Blasphemy	4. Meekness
5. Vulgar language (mouth)	5. Longsuffering
6. Lying	6. Love

When you answer to God is "Yes" and you want to please him, you are committing to replacing evil thoughts from your mindset so that God can fill you with his righteousness.

The enemy (Satan) plans and schemes and devious ways to get into your mindset, remember this is his number one plot, get the mind and get the person. Remember our story about Eve in the garden, which is always his first step to disrupt the mind and control it. Determine you will win this battle of your mind. In Romans 8:6 "For to be carnally minded is death; but to be spiritually minded is life and peace. To stay spiritually minded it will take all your effort, all your time to maintain this new mind. In II Corinthians 5:17 "Therefore if any man be in Christ, he is a new creature: old things are passed away; behold, all things are become new." Choose to police your mindset every day, by depositing his word in your heart, so that your thoughts can be in spiritual alignment with his will. All humanity needs to bring order into their chaotic thoughts. Desire to be more like Jesus. Take Godly pleasure in studying his word, praying, fasting, and dedicating your total self for his glorification. The rewards are impressive, peace, joy, and his contentment can be yours, but you must exercise spiritual stamina to keep your mind on Christ daily.

CHAPTER 13

ORDER IN OUR HEART

Our physical heart is the most important vital organ in our body. It pumps streams of blood and allows oxygen to travel to the important systems in our body. When the heart has a major problem, many things begin to happen to our bodies and may need heart surgery. Well! When our spiritual heart is filled with all kinds of wickedness and sinfulness it produces hardness to hearing the voice of the living God. We are to concentrate on being sensitive to the voice of God. In Hebrews 3:7-8 "Wherefore (as the Holy Ghost saith, Today if ye will hear his voice, Harden not your hearts, as in the provocation, in the day of temptation in the wilderness:" Who was he talking to here? The house of Israel. his nation of Jews. Today, we have the greatest power to help us overcome sin if we allow ourselves to be led by the Holy Ghost. God is calling us to turn our hearts, rend our hearts from evil and submit to his will.

In Joel 2:13 "And rend your heart, and not your garments, and turn unto the LORD your God: for he is gracious and merciful, slow to anger, and of great kindness, and repenteth him of the evil." What is God telling us here in this important verse? The word "rend" to remove from its place, to tear apart. Just saying "I am sorry," is not appropriate, God is looking for repenting from the deceitfulness of sin that was bound in our heart.

The lifestyle of sin is full of deceitfulness. In Hebrews 3:13 "But exhort one another daily, while it is called Today; lest any of you be hardened through the deceitfulness of sin." Our will, our heart, and our mind work in unison, when we do not yield to sin, we produce the fruits of righteousness. But when we yield to sin it produces all kinds of works of the flesh.

In Jeremiah 17:9-10 "The heart is deceitful above all things, and desperately wicked: who can know it? I the LORD search the heart, I try the reins, even to give every man according to his ways, and according to the fruit of his doings." God is calling humanity to change their ways and become converted from their lifestyle of sin.

Each person on this planet earth was born in sin. Yes! we all at one time or the other allowed our sin "nature" to reign in us. We would try desperately to stop doing those terrible things, but we found ourselves again and again doing evil. In Romans 6:16 "Know ye not, that to whom ye yield yourselves servants to obey, his servants ye are to whom ye obey; whether of sin unto death, or of obedience unto righteousness?" We have (2) choices here, whether we yield to sin or obedience to righteousness. When we yield, we are giving over to whatever power is greater in our lives. In the Amplified Bible version its rendition of Romans 6:13 gives us a more definitive viewpoint, "Do not continue offering or yielding your bodily members [and faculties] to sin as instruments (tools) of wickedness.

But offer and yield yourselves to God as though you have been raised from the dead to [perpetual] life, and your bodily members [and faculties] to God, presenting them as implements of righteousness." When you chronically live under the bondage of sin and seek no deliverance you instantly become a slave to sin. You have allowed the spiritual chains and bondages to take a whole of your mind and heart. That is why we need to hear and obey the gospel message of salvation, which is our answer to spiritual deliverance. In Romans 6:17 "But God be thanked, that ye were the servants of sin, but ye have obeyed from the heart that form of doctrine which was delivered you.

We needed a solution to rectify our sin problem. God sent his only begotten son Jesus to provide a remedy. Jesus paid the penalty of our sin and took upon himself the judgment of our sin. Sometimes we get involved in circumstances beyond our control. We may feel like there is no way for us to get untangled in the bondages we may have created for ourselves or that was brought on by other individuals. There is a way to get free and stay free. Accepting Jesus as Lord and Savior offers you a fantastic opportunity to become part of God's Kingdom family. God wants us free from torment, free from oppression and fear. You have the power to control what goes into your mind. When you guard the portals of your conscience, will and spirit, you value what is deposited in you.

Letting His word, His ways and doing His will, will help you become the free Christian you are called to be.

Your heart should be your treasure chest. A treasure chest holds precious and valuable things. If there are good seeds of the word of God in your heart, you will produce fruits of righteousness. Luke 6:45 "A good man out of the good treasure of his heart bringeth forth that which is good; and an evil man out of the evil treasure of his heart bringeth forth that which is evil: for of the abundance of the heart his mouth speaketh."

The Psalmist clearly stated in 119:11 "Thy word have I hid in mine heart, that I might not sin against thee." If you love His word, you will protect and value it, so that it can dwell in you richly. You cherish his word, and you honor its principles and doctrines. God's word is so powerful. In the Amplified Bible version Hebrews 4:12 "For the Word that God speaks is alive and full of power [making it active] operative, energizing, and effective]; it is sharper than any two-edged sword, [penetrating to the dividing line of the breath of life (soul) and [the immortal] spirit and of joints and marrow [of the deepest parts of our nature], exposing and sifting and analyzing and judging the very thoughts and purposes of the heart."

Everything that we have discussed in our lesson on Order the Mind we have given you good important insights to consider.

Whether you are a believer or just starting your spiritual relationship, know that God wants to order your steps, God wants to plant your footsteps so that you can fulfill your destiny as God foresees. We want our God to be pleased with our life, we want to be a benefit as a Christians in our community, We want our families to be blessed, so that the light of his glorious gospel can win them to church, and therefore bringing in the harvest of souls for our local churches.

CHAPTER 14

REJOICE AND CELEBRATE THE NEW YOU

Psalms 118:24

This is the day which the LORD hath made; we will rejoice and be glad in it."

You have a new sense of happiness, you can now rejoice, the spirit of joy is resting on you, because you have chosen to allow God's hand to touch you. You have taken all of your past and laid it aside, all your sins are forgiven, the weight and burden are no more upon your heart. Your mind is renewed, your heart is changed, and you are walking in the will of God.

Each and every day is a new day of expectation, because now you are a new son/daughter in Christ. Your days are no longer under the snare of the enemy (Satan), you have experienced a miracle of new life. There is no greater joy in the world than that of having a relationship with Jesus Christ.

When you consider where God has brought you from, the pain, the losses, the trials, all the sufferings, your heart leaps for joy. You feel no guilt or condemnation in Amplified Bible Version Romans 8:1 "Therefore, [there is] now no condemnation (no adjudging guilty of wrong) for those who are in Christ Jesus, who live [and] walk not after the dictates of the flesh, but after the dictates of the

Spirit." When you know that you are free from judgment, free from condemnation, you feel a great sign of relief. No more mental and emotional anguish. Jesus took away all your sins cast them away as far as the east is from the west. Forgiveness is God's gift to you for your total confession of sin.

There is a wonderful story of repentance in Psalms 51 written by King David who committed his sin and prayed for forgiveness. This is the only Psalm that mentions the Holy Spirit (free spirit). King David, warrior, the musical harpist, the poetic writer of Psalms expressing God's sovereignty, was a mere man that loved God. Let us dig deep into this penitential Psalm.

David admits no more games, O' Lord God I need mercy Psalm 51:1 "Have mercy upon me, O God, according to thy loving kindness according unto the multitude of thy tender mercies blot out my transgressions."

David was not excusing his actions, no one to blame but his own lustful behavior. This is the right thing to do, it is "my" sin. Did David deserve mercy? No, in man's estimation, but Yes, in the eyes of God. Yet, he was crying, begging for God's mercy. Oh, yes, there was a penalty for adultery, a grave penalty. Mercy in the Greek translation is "eleos" taken from the word olive oil, and in Hebrew mercy is "hesed" steadfast love. David wanted God's eternal loving kindness; he wanted to feel the soothing, comfort and healing power of his steadfast love.

David asked because he knew his God renders tender mercies and he would blot out his sins from the book, according to Old Testament era.

Psalm 51:2 "Wash me thoroughly from mine iniquity, and cleanse me from my sin. David's confession was seasoned with remorse and sorrow. David owned up to his sin "mine." Yes, I confess it, but I need your help O Lord. David wanted the dirtiness of sin removed, Oh God! please remove it from his life.

Psalm 51:3 "For I acknowledge my transgressions: and my sin is ever before me." David's 2nd admission "my" sin. David said I will not hide it any longer, because it is a constant reminder of my adultery.

Psalm 51:4 "Against thee, thee only, have I sinned, and done this evil in thy sight: that thy mightiest be justified when thou speakest, and be clear when thou judgest." David's confession to God, yes, I knew the law, I sinned against you God. I cannot hide behind it, you see my evil, O Lord declare me righteous again, do not judge me as man would judge me.

Psalm 51:5 "Behold, I was shapen in iniquity; and in sin did my mother conceive me." This sin business was initiated when Adam disobeyed and transgressed the commandment affecting all future generations. Jesus died on the cross to paid the penalty and judgment of humanity's sins.

In I Peter 2:24 "Who his own self bare our sins in his own body on the tree, (cross) that we, being dead to sins, should live unto righteousness: by whose stripes ye were healed."

Psalm 51:6 "Behold, thou desirest truth in the inward parts: and in the hidden part thou shalt make me to know wisdom."

David knew now that lying would no longer be his cover-up. God sees his heart now, like an open book, searching for a note of truth, some note of brokenness and a sincere heart. David knew that his steps, needed order, so that he could receive the divine wisdom of God to give him freedom and healing redemption.

Psalm 51:7 "Purge me with hyssop, and I shall be clean: wash me, and I shall be whiter than snow." "Hyssop was a plant that the priests used to remove a stain. David wanted to be put back in his righteous state of mind; he no longer wanted to see the images of his sin in his mind. David knew that his way to being redeemed required a process. Our redemption was Jesus blood that took away our sins and forever forgiven.

Psalm 51: 8 "Make me to hear joy and gladness; that at the bones which thou hast broken may rejoice." David's breakthrough of being free from the guilt of his sin was the result of his humility and love for God to do what was right in his sight.

Psalm 51:12 "Restore unto me the joy of thy salvation; and uphold me with thy free spirit." David loved God with all his heart, and his sincerity was reflected in his undeserving request. David, I want it now, I want that joy unspeakable full of your glory and allow me to experience your salvation. David said do not take your Holy Spirit (free spirit) from me, I need your free spirit every day of my life.

David's confession of sin and example of humility was written for all humanity because God knew we would fall short of his glory. In Romans 3:23 "For all have sinned and come short of the glory of God;" God so loved the world that he gave his only son. St. John 3:16 "For God so loved the world, that he gave his only begotten Son, that whosoever believeth in him should not perish, but have everlasting life."

This story of David is not a dream, it is a reality and truth of what life is about when you fall. God is right there to pick you up and put the pieces of your life back together. No matter who you are, where you come from, God has an ultimate plan, an order of steps that he has outlined for your spiritual life. You must not miss this opportunity to come to fellowship, to allow his presence to abide in your life and experience all the joys of salvation. God has so many blessings that he wants to give you, turn your life over to Jesus. Repent of your ways so that you can become the Christian, he wants you to be.

Accommodate his plan for your life say "Yes" to participate in the water baptism and infilling of the Holy Spirit. You will be able to testify about God's goodness in your life.

God wants to use you to be his witness for your family, in your community, on your job so that you can win souls for his Kingdom of light. Answer the call of "Yes" today and forever, so that you can walk in your true destiny, God wants to order your footsteps, "Come and follow him to enjoy His glorious destiny for you.

CHAPTER 15

FINALITY OF GOD'S ORDER REVELATION

We have come down to the concluding chapter of our book titled "The Day I say "Yes" Order my Steps Dear God. It has been a wonderful literary journey that has opened our theme from Manna Nation Ministries for the new year of 2024, Order my Steps- A Return to Divine Order. We have traveled the path of Order and discussed the excellent foundations of how God can miraculously rearrange and change individuals for his divine will and purpose.

Humanity's destination has a beginning and an ending, which we have discussed in our chapters and why order is important in one's spiritual life. As we follow God's steps and stay in the correct path, our obedience will reward us with the final and awesome blessing, that is fulfilling our ultimate desire to spend eternity with our Lord.

I highly recommend that you, my readers and believers, keep this prophetic scripture always in your treasure chest of valuable words.

I Corinthians 2:9 "But as it is written, Eye hath not seen, nor ear heard, neither have entered into the heart of man, the things which God hath prepared for them that love him."

John, the apostle, and writer of the book of Revelation, was the only person that God revealed all the visions and preparations of our eternal home.

God always has the perfect answer for our query, he is a God that is "omniscience." This important description of God's infinite mind comes from the Latin word "all" and Scientia meaning "knowledge," or the state of knowing everything. Who else but our only true and living God could engineer this great wonderful blessing?

All around the world there are 8 wonders to behold namely Tajmahal in Agra, India, The Great Wall of China in Beijing, The Christ the Redeemer Statue in Rio de Janeiro, Machu Picchu in Peru, Chichen Itza in Mexico's Yucatan Peninsula, The Roman Coliseum in Rome, Petra (Jordan) and Angkor Wat. These are all beautiful, but they are only significant in the earthly realm built by man. Our God has created a new city in all its finery of precious stones and pearls and a street of gold. In Revelation 21:5 "And he that sat upon the throne said, Behold, I make all things new. And he said unto me, Write: for these words are true and faithful:

When humanity plunged into a state of sin, God had to provide a Redeemer, Jesus Christ to be our connection to God, whereas he reconciled us to meet with God. Herein, we have various meeting and dwelling places for the presence of God.

In the Old Testament we had the Tabernacle, we had the Solomon's Temple, In the New Testament we have Jesus Christ and the church and now looking forward in the future the city of the New Jerusalem. In this new holy city, there will be no need for a temple. In Revelations 21:22 "And I (John) saw no temple therein: for the Lord God Almighty and the Lamb are the temple of it."

God created humanity with a physical body that was ordained and purposed for a spiritual temple.

In I Corinthians 3:17 "If any man defile the temple of God, him shall God destroy; for the temple of God is holy, which temple ye are." Our physical churches are God's house where his glory and presence is experienced; our new eternal dwelling place will be a combination of heaven and earth. In Revelation 21:1 "And I saw a new heaven and a new earth: for the first heaven and the first earth were passed away; and there was no more sea." What was in the beginning, in the creation, the book of Genesis, no form, darkness and void is now restored to its original glory. In this new holy city, John heard a voice echoing in Revelation 21:3 "And I heard a great voice out of heaven saying, Behold the tabernacle of God is with men, and he will dwell with then, and they shall be his people, and God himself shall be with them, and be their God". The tabernacle (foreshadow the coming of Jesus Christ) was a place symbolizing the presence of God.

God wants men to seek and worship him, In John 4:23 "But the hour cometh, and now is, when the true worshippers shall worship the Father in spirit and in truth: for the Father seeketh such to worship him" This new holy city will be a dwelling place of peace and harmony, The believers, the nations and Israel will be a part of this wonderful and magnificent place of glory. We will have a pure river of water of life, clear as crystal. Now you know some of our water channels are poisoned with disease, which requires us to buy filters to drink it, but the throne of God and of the Lamb we will have endless, eternal crystal-clear water of life. Not only that but we will be able to live forever and forever because we will have a tree of life. There shall be no more curse, we shall finally see his face and his name shall be in our foreheads. (Revelation 22:1-4) For now until that great getting up morning when the dead in Christ and the believers are snatched away. We will not be subject to the wrath and judgment of God upon the earth. It has been over 2000 years and humanity is still departing from the beliefs and standards of the living word of God. Yes! there are souls being still saved all across the country and nations, because we hear of the testimonies of the harvest of souls in our churches. The world will continue sleepily in their slumber of sin, bewitched and living under the snare and bondage of the enemy of Satan. God has in his heart of mercy; compassion sent his preachers and teachers to preach the gospel message.

Their Holy Ghost anointing and power showing signs, wonders, and miracles as evidence of God's power has proven that we serve a true and living God. We have the one invitation that Jesus recorded in the Holy Bible a verse of compelling testimony. In Revelation 22:16-17 "I Jesus have sent mine angel to testify unto you these things in the churches, I am the root and the offspring of David, and the bright and morning star. And the Spirit and the bride say, Come. And let him that heareth say, Come. And let him that is athirst come. And whosoever will; let him take the water of life freely." The invitation has been spoken out of the mouth of Jesus, why not consider coming to him "Today and Say "Yes" Order my Steps Dear God, you will not regret the marvelous metamorphosis that will happen in your earthly life to an ordered life connected to God.

RESOURCES

The Full Life Study Bible, KJV The New Testament, 1990 Fiverr Seller Services

Merriam Webster's s Collegiate Dictionary 10th edition 1994 Thompson Chain Reference Bible, KJV

The New Strong's Complete Dictionary of Bible Words, James Strong, L.L.D., S.T.D

The Annotated Study Bible, KJV, 1983

The Amplified Bible containing Old and New Testament (Amplified) 1987

OTHER BOOKS
AUTHORED AND PUBLISHED BY
JACQUELINE COATES

All books are available on:
Amazon.com

Contact:
Elder Jacqueline Coates
tcsservices59@gmail.com